The New York Times

Super Saturday Crosswords

THE HARDEST CROSSWORD OF THE WEEK

Edited by Will Shortz

ST. MARTIN'S GRIFFIN ❧ NEW YORK

The New York Times

Super Saturday Crosswords

1

ACROSS

1 Kind of publishing
8 Car buyer's concern
15 Nonresident doctor: Var.
16 Italian rice dish
17 "Fowl" language?
19 She loves in Latin
20 Suckle
21 Sign on
22 Cooper novel, with "The"
23 E.T.S. offering
24 Mop topper
25 Part of G.E.: Abbr.
27 It's an old story
29 "Bye-bye"
30 Go for more oil
32 Stored some hay
34 Author Kobo of Japan
35 Take notes
36 Victims in a Bologna sculpture
40 Mariner's guide
44 President Arthur's middle name
45 Hang around
47 Table salt
48 Puzzle fodder: Abbr.
49 ___ chi (meditative exercises)
50 Juno, but not Jupiter
51 Hard to grasp
53 Simile start
55 Can-opener targets
56 Way to mumble 17-Across
59 Attic function
60 Early worker?
61 Kind of proverbial pole
62 Rests under a sombrero

DOWN

1 He'll humiliate you
2 Role model, e.g.
3 Wandered off
4 Lane lover?
5 Make a federal case of?
6 ___ impulse
7 Quick read
8 Bridge support
9 Ready enough
10 "___ was saying . . ."
11 Does once?
12 Leading the good life
13 Say again
14 Reporter's book
18 Unexciting
26 Business-news publisher Keith

27 Arms in the water?
28 Use with relish
29 Business big shot
31 ___ Saud
33 Roman Helios
36 Carpenter's floor cover
37 Pasta style
38 Book-to-movie words
39 Faux wool
40 Altar egos
41 Glowing
42 Summer cooler
43 Knifes.
46 It might turn over a new leaf
52 Broadway showing, for short
53 NBC's peacock, e.g.

54 Shelter: Fr.
55 Napoopoo neckwear
57 P. V. Narasimha ___, Indian P.M.
58 ___ Dawn Chong

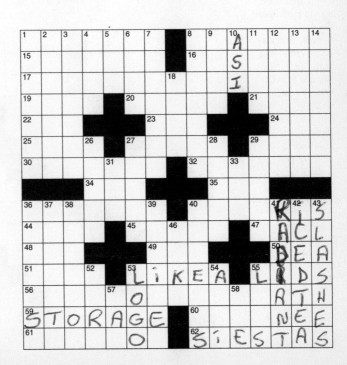

2

by Glenton Petgrave

ACROSS

1 Puget Sound city
7 Escorts of a sort
14 Left out
15 Away doing research, e.g.
16 Went by car
17 Raises the hem
19 Sassy
20 "Not guilty by reason of insanity," e.g.
21 Sticky place?
22 Wraps up
23 T, for one
24 Odium
25 Willis's "___ Hard"
26 Make up (for)
27 Word after flip or tip
28 Warmhearted
30 Ward off
32 Lover who lived by the Hellespont
33 Swing music
35 Crawls, in a way
38 Alecto, Megaera and Tisiphone
40 Actress Dawber
41 Added muscle, with "up"
42 Answers for Nanette?
45 Tennyson's "Geraint and ___"
47 Gators' kin
48 Madras dress
49 Voting nay
50 Sign of a saint
51 Aired again
52 Not setting the agenda
54 Kind of room or legend
55 Soft-shell clam
56 Repay, in a way
57 Not in so many words?
58 F.T.C. subject

DOWN

1 Bedeviled
2 Reuners
3 Charleston college, with "The"
4 Aromas
5 Athletic event
6 Connect
7 A little gander?
8 Exist naturally
9 Show impolite satisfaction
10 "___ the ramparts . . ."
11 Door closer
12 Was gluttonous
13 Barbara Boxer, for one
18 Won all the races
20 Record player
23 Paint can direction
26 Welcomes
29 A little resistance?
30 Cupidinous
31 Churchill's sign
33 Snowbird
34 Wraths
35 Asparagus unit
36 Most sick-looking
37 Be a copycat
38 Tom's behavior?
39 Entangling
41 Go places
43 Holland's royal family
44 Literature Nobelist, 1978
46 Food-cubing gizmo
47 Ding-dong
48 Split up
51 Use a cleaver
53 Words of gratitude
54 Flight from justice

3

ACROSS

1 Kind of race or queen
5 ___ point
10 Malign
14 Morning wind personified
15 Rocket stage
16 Actress Sedgwick
17 End of "America the Beautiful," in brief
20 Circus workers
21 All-purpose song lyrics
22 Society page word
23 Put on board
24 1987 #1 hit by Heart
26 Playmate
29 Learned
33 Success story
38 To be, in Paree
39 Beatitudes phrase, in brief
43 Cotton pod
44 They're alphabetized in phone directories
45 Books that suffer where and tear?
49 Queensland neighbor: Abbr.
50 Customs
52 Broadway's Harold
56 1981 Blake Edwards comedy
59 Plaster backing
60 Thermoplastics
62 Event of 12/16/1773, in brief
65 Deputy
66 Actress Verdugo
67 Debt satisfier
68 Winning margin, maybe
69 Haggadah reading occasion
70 Peeved

DOWN

1 Unhinged
2 Part of R.E.A.
3 Bouquet
4 Staked
5 Congratulates in a way
6 Kind of mania
7 Inventer Nikola
8 Take a drag on
9 Shakespeare's Robin Starveling
10 Schuss
11 Boston suburb
12 Push for
13 Iditarod, e.g.
18 Brunch fare
19 Part of Mork's sign-off
25 Swelling
27 ___ atque vale
28 Ruled
30 Particular
31 Math diagram
32 Comic screams
33 Palindromic pop group
34 Coagulate
35 "The Divine Comedy" locale
36 Arabic word meaning "submission"
37 B.&O., and others
40 Large wine cask
41 Nolte's "48 ___"
42 Bundle up
46 Tutti's opposite, in music
47 Does away with
48 Finalize
51 Like some horses
53 Feared exams
54 Linguist Pei
55 Register
56 Saxophonist Getz
57 Columbus's home
58 Some of them are twins
60 Wisher's sight
61 New Year's word
63 Busy one
64 Ship's heading

4

by Manny Nosowsky

ACROSS

1 Longtime New Yorker cartoonist
10 Doctors' professional magazine
14 Kind of booth
15 Business department
16 Fan
17 Typical subjects in a psych study
18 Grilling spots
19 Beach item
20 Unhappy crowd sound
21 Spanish quarters
22 Number five iron
26 Taken in a sedan
27 Llama herder, once
28 Lots
32 Kaiser kin
33 In a blah manner
34 Gambler's game
35 Means of support?
37 Bee's landing platform
38 Rockwell and Clark
39 Buying a quart of milk, e.g.
40 Star attractions?
43 Zetterling of "All Those Tomorrows"
44 Excise
45 Short hole, perhaps
50 In readiness
51 Go to bed
52 Fur pieces
53 Exactly
54 Last column in addition
55 In need of exorcism

DOWN

1 Tut-tut
2 This: Sp.
3 Lawsuit basis
4 "___ Coming" (1969 pop hit)
5 Makes lots, as money
6 "Don't be such ___!"
7 Mob scenes
8 Entre ___
9 Thunder Bay prov.
10 Candy store purchase
11 Court defense
12 ___ Park
13 Fools
15 Literary Laurence
19 Have a ball
21 Bubbles
22 Neighbor of 9-Down
23 San Francisco founder
24 Have a look-see
25 "School" lessons?
26 Chicago five
28 Call it ___
29 VHS alternative
30 Words before instant or uproar
31 Blabbed
33 He went through Hell
36 Giants coach Dan
37 Please, to Shakespeare
39 Kipling's "When ___ Last Picture Is Painted"
40 Advertising film
41 Prominent Red Square name
42 Chemical compound
43 Dillon and Biondi
45 Spanish conifer
46 They peck at their food
47 Greek letters
48 The life of Riley
49 Gave the once-over
51 Short trip

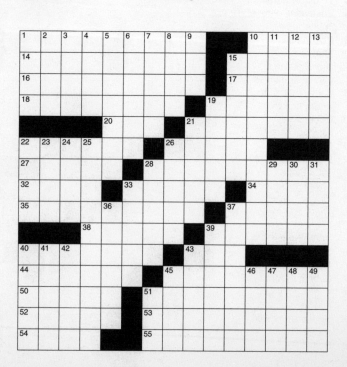

5

by Rand H. Burns

ACROSS

1 Hayes of "Shaft"
6 Literary monogram
9 Restaurateur Vincent
14 Edgartown's locale
17 Food processor?
18 Piquer du ___ (nose-dive)
19 Totally rad, in teen talk
20 "Does she or doesn't she?" mystery
21 Mira or Vega
22 Sweeping hairstyle
24 More inadequate
26 Tries again
29 Bode
30 Act of bending back
32 Lash
33 Pipsqueaks
34 Dispirited
35 "Let's vary piracee with a little ___": W. S. Gilbert
37 Stole
38 They run before dinner
39 Crooked
40 Medicine Nobelist ___ von Behring
41 Hoover employee?
42 Cold's kin
45 More obstreperous
47 Lanka leader
50 Grimm tale
53 Trials
54 Dick and Schick, e.g.
55 Indicator of 22-kt. gold
56 90-degree headings

DOWN

1 Model who told of Somalia's plight
2 Unloading time?
3 ZIP codes starting 85- and 86-: Abbr.
4 PIN-dependent source of funds
5 Con man
6 Poly ending
7 Trouper Gardner et al.
8 Whirl
9 Virginia in 1861
10 Granada governess
11 South African money
12 Cart
13 Fainéant
15 Camp David guest, 1978
16 Lolitas
21 Shirk duties?
23 Healthful cereal choice
24 Dillies
25 Ancient bazaar
26 French President Coty and others
27 Upset
28 Overly sentimental
29 Lackland or Lowry, for short
30 "Aw shucks" and "Gee whillikers," e.g.
31 Open fabric
33 Chef Boyardee serving
36 Artists
37 Medicinal paper strips
39 Offputting fish?
41 Cleaning for military inspection
42 Toss and turn
43 Elegance
44 They cover all the bases
46 Leave in
47 Travels between the poles?
48 Major flare-up
49 Travel guide listings
51 Stroke
52 Amtrak stop: Abbr.

6

by Manny Nosowsky

ACROSS

1 Hunt
6 Dos follower
12 Asseveration
14 When the ghost appears in "Hamlet"
15 Cold weather wear
17 Name
18 ___ out of (reject)
19 Famously hot California town
21 Like some tapes
22 First name in fashion
24 Longtime labor chief
25 Matter of meter
26 Former Israeli P.M.
28 Catch
29 Sheep menace
30 San Francisco landmark
33 Not the world's nicest boss
34 Smuggler's nemesis, maybe
35 Personal article, in law
36 Two ___
37 Bit of regatta
41 "Blue Moon" lyricist
42 Hasidic leader
44 Like some medicines
45 Classified item, for short
46 Pitches
48 Telephone button
49 Tar
51 Walter Raleigh quest
53 City on the Willamette
54 Tripoli locale
55 Discharged
56 Work clothes, perhaps

DOWN

1 Use a Swingline
2 Checker, maybe
3 Olympic abbr.
4 Portray
5 Pay homage to
6 Bates
7 They're good with tricks
8 Engine additive
9 Remembrance of things past?
10 Active
11 Is conscientious
12 News first
13 Stuff it!
16 1975 Pulitzer playwright
20 50-cent picture
23 "Scram!"
25 Opera set in Seville
27 Lion's amount?
29 Matter of course?
31 Palindromic lady
32 Churchill, e.g.
33 Want
34 Work out at the gym
35 Fox-hunt sites
38 Blass rival
39 ___ House
40 Crazy as ___
42 Blew a fuse
43 Over
46 Sprinkle site
47 "___ it" (conversation closer)
50 Frost relative
52 Streaked

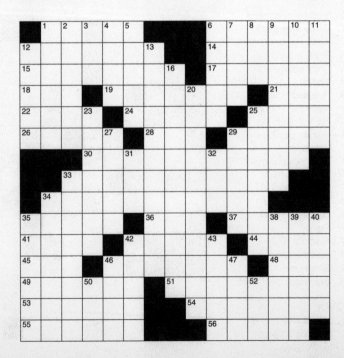

7 — *by Rand H. Burns*

ACROSS

1. Fix
6. Rat ___
10. "Sanford and Son" producer
14. "Blue ___" (1977 hit)
15. Secret advisers
17. Vowel mark
18. One of five related names in this puzzle
19. Glimpse
21. Snuggery
22. Buoyant one
25. ___ à cheval (horseshoe)
26. Ancestor of the Edomites
30. Timeplace?
31. Actress Talbot
33. Secure
35. Kind of road
38. Linguistic origins
39. See 18-Across
41. Bake, in a way
43. Title
46. Factory seconds, for short
48. Cruising
49. Reconstruction, for one
50. No frill, this
51. Architectural crossette
53. Downsized upright
55. Decorate
57. Undulant ones
58. See 18-Across
62. Futurist Toffler
66. Turkey
67. Green
68. Declared items
69. Slowly sinks
70. Formicary denizen

DOWN

1. Recession
2. Mangle
3. Kind of tooth
4. Hugo contender
5. See 18-Across
6. Bruised
7. Crux
8. Commodious
9. Olympics skier McKinney
10. Gilbert works
11. Ransom Olds's middle name
12. ___ American
13. "The Facts of Life" star
16. Charles, e.g.
20. Rap sheet blot
22. Patch
23. 12-foot bird
24. Move to act
25. Travel incentive
27. Pourer's request
28. Ready-fire link
29. Spanish article
32. Kind of shell
34. See 18-Across
36. Mercenaries
37. McGrew and others
40. Hall of Fame Dodger
41. Kind of tax
42. Initials in old Europe
44. Vexation
45. Well-rehearsed
47. Stage actress Marian
52. C'est ___
54. "Satanic Verses" topic
56. Class
57. Vanities
58. Vane dir.
59. Bake sale org., perhaps
60. Auto option
61. "Wayne's World" exclamation
63. Life
64. Secret follower
65. Aerialist's safeguard

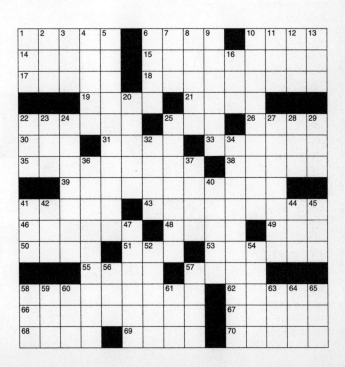

8

by Manny Nosowsky

ACROSS

1. ___ Tuesday
7. Drools
15. Neologist
16. Survivable
17. "The Newton of Electricity"
18. Neil Armstrong commanded it
19. Maintain one's credit rating?
20. Where to warm one's bones
21. Popular dress cut
22. Gorge
23. Demoted maj.
24. Charlie Chan portrayer
25. Crossword bird
26. Wacko
27. Bandleader Lewis
28. Raise one's spirits, perhaps
30. Show horse
33. Driving forces
34. Flower tops
38. Blurrer
39. Man of la Mancha
40. "Say again?"
42. Wept over
43. Mast rope
44. Indiana ___
46. Get ahead
47. Nukes
48. "We ___ no thin red 'eroes": Kipling
49. Make a decision
50. Small
51. Waits for a better offer
53. Woolgatherer's topic
54. Cheer
55. Aspen's relative
56. Kind of care
57. Part of the Ralik Chain

DOWN

1. Muni or Pacino role
2. Follow the signal?
3. Undulant
4. "The Bad News Bears" star
5. V.I.P. section?
6. Earlier than
7. "Make it ___!"
8. Memorable Eddie of the Yankees
9. She wrote "Grapefruit"
10. Note above A
11. This should never be stuffed
12. French star
13. Precipitated
14. Less up front
20. Most sound
23. Sorrows
26. Native New Mexican
29. He once had a hand in morning TV
30. Let go, in a way
31. Where Joan of Arc burned
32. Parched
35. Nohow
36. Not run-of-the-mill
37. Encounter Hollywood or Holyfield?
40. "Satires" author
41. World group based in Paris
42. Climber's descent
44. Legends are made there
45. Inscribed pillar
46. Brie's tray-mate
47. Marx-man
50. Novel action
52. Took a load off
53. Psychiatrists' org.

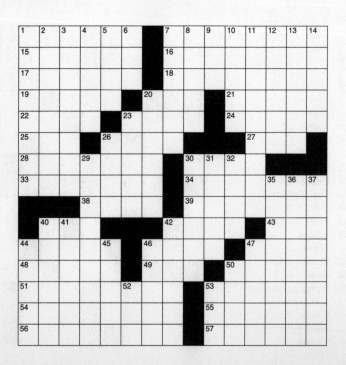

9

ACROSS

1 Hans Arp style
5 Swindle
9 Sternward
14 Short jacket
15 Ballerina Spessivtseva
16 "Morning Glory" bloom
17 Friend of Antony in "Antony and Cleopatra"
19 Waiting, in a way
20 Walking __
21 Katharina's match in "The Taming of the Shrew"
23 Tiny protest
25 Selene's sister
26 Fictional planet
27 Blowout
30 Mama on "That's My Mama"
33 Mess
34 Home to Tell
35 Big name in toys
39 Ruby defender
41 Workout site
43 1984 political diarist
44 Searches thoroughly
46 Muff
48 Campaign award
49 Sunrooms
51 Author Victoria
52 __ glance
55 Approval
56 Candidate of '08
58 Son of Duncan in "Macbeth"
61 Arcade name
65 Bye-bye
66 Hotspur ally in "Henry IV, Part I"
68 Martin Sheen's real first name
69 Conoco rival
70 "99 Luftballons" singer
71 Appraising
72 Be smart
73 Heaven on Earth

DOWN

1 "Whip it" group
2 Ancient disk
3 Flor of film
4 Twin in "The Comedy of Errors"
5 Farm land
6 Barbershop item
7 Fever
8 Original
9 Unplugged?
10 Court seat
11 Granting that
12 See 63-Down
13 Pillow stuffing
18 Its root is pride according to Chaucer
22 Muddy
24 Crossword bird
27 Old dos
28 Anchovy sauce
29 Titan's home
31 Redder, perhaps
32 Clown in "As You Like it"
36 Start of a legal plea
37 Pianist Gilels
38 Treasures
40 Respirator
42 Drought
45 Pig
47 "The Facts of Life" star
50 Saws
52 Antarctic cape
53 Currently
54 Tropical resins
57 Nefarious
59 Many millennia
60 She requested "As Time Goes By"
62 Gaping, maybe
63 "And Then There Were None" director, with 12-Down
64 Kerman locale
67 Rebuffs

ACROSS

1 "Hide in Plain Sight" star
10 Drumbeat
14 Briefly
15 Yammer
16 "My ___" (1972 hit)
17 Preminger classic
18 Never ever
19 Submit
20 It clinks in drinks
21 Pretends not to see
22 Trump Castle, for one
26 Whitman bloomer
27 Behind, in a way
28 A number 1
32 Way to go
33 Hardly laid-back
34 Horse play?
35 Startling revelation
37 Pebble Beach contest
38 1967 Uris novel
39 Junior rocker
40 Blitzes with a blizzard
43 ___ kwon do
44 Nicholson film "Drive, ___"
45 Bent
50 Wax Websterian
51 Browne of "Black Like Me"
52 Moves cautiously
53 Irish Sea spot
54 Henna handler
55 Lombardi lecture

DOWN

1 Novelty hit of 1919
2 Working hard
3 "The Magic Mountain" author
4 Breakfast brand
5 Scheduling
6 Like Eugene Field's cat
7 Lively, in Lyon
8 Teen trauma
9 Battery term.
10 "Pocketful of Miracles" director
11 Eulogizes
12 Places in the heart
13 "I ___ what I said"
15 Two-dimensional
19 Imagist poet Doolittle
21 Squeegee
22 Rise to the occasion
23 On the road
24 Planned setting
25 Steaming?
26 "If I Had a Hammer" singer

28 "Oh! Calcutta!" co-writer
29 Couples club
30 Upwardly mobile Israeli group?
31 Multiday building project?
33 Lukewarm
36 Nosegays
37 Make beforehand, as rice
39 Scrub
40 Like some horses
41 Square
42 Orange or Indian
43 Radio pioneer
45 Swanky
46 Avoirdupois
47 Michigan college town
48 1963 Best Actress
49 Six-mile-plus run

51 Ocasek of the Cars

by Rand H. Burns

ACROSS

1 With cunning
7 Track clothes
12 Queen Liliuokalani song
13 Groovy
15 Storing fodder
16 Wagner's birthplace
17 "Fear and Trembling" writer
19 Patagonian locale: Abbr.
20 Dark horse
21 Vixen's master
23 Fifth Avenue outfit
26 Able, facetiously
28 Game of five hundred
31 Overcome
32 Saline seven
34 Theorist
35 "Bleak House" girl
36 He upset T.E.D.
37 Barkeep's request
39 British container
40 Large in scope
42 Sharpen
44 Info on 37-Across
45 Like some payments
47 Establishment
48 Author Rule and others
49 Parlays, e.g.
51 Mossy
53 Terrorist Nidal
55 Lamebrain
60 Pilfer
62 Frayed
63 Dead Sea Scrolls preservers
64 Do over and over
65 Revelrous parties
66 Goddess in a chariot

DOWN

1 Et ___
2 Star's vehicle
3 Lines across a circle
4 Matsuo Basho work
5 Isolation
6 Peterman
7 Uncle Toby's creator
8 Precious metals
9 Kind of stick
10 New U.N. member of 1992
11 Move
12 Pump, in a way
13 Batten
14 Good fellow
18 Fictional terrier
22 Hosp. sect. for cardiac cases
23 Pundit
24 Actor Quinn
25 Kind of sandwich
27 St. ___ (vacation spot)
29 Rule
30 Piscatory birds
33 Convey via Amesian
36 City at the mouth of the Pearl River
38 Forsaken
41 Calm waters site
43 Platter
46 Contests
48 Stick
50 Bank woes
52 Gauge reading
53 Highly excited, in slang
54 Smack
56 Alternative name for 21-Across
57 Spirit
58 Das ___ (the old): Ger.
59 Chromotrope
61 Shepherd's place

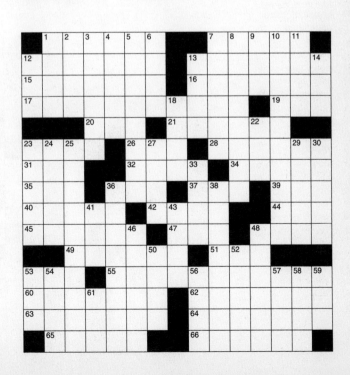

by Rand H. Burns

ACROSS

1 French composer Francis
8 Silent "ugh"
15 Kind of eclipse
16 Of a son's love
17 Stipulation
18 Narrow at the base, as leaves
19 Left command
20 Affording rest
22 Broadside
23 Potent leader
25 Letters in a 60's cigarette ad
26 Sub outlet
27 Dog-tired
29 Oft-repeated sound of reproof
30 W.W. II general and namesakes
31 Euphemistic oath of old
33 Longtime Israeli statesman
35 Dodge
36 Seneca foe
37 Salesman's line
39 1969 Luchino Visconti film, with "The"
42 Dessert introduced in 1897
43 Apply
45 Leave just the kitchen sink?
47 Host
48 "___ Irish Rose"
50 Dance to chants
51 Mauna ___
52 Went ape
54 Liked loads
55 Jesus' tongue
57 Descendant of Esau
59 Coach of the Nittany Lions
60 Countervailing force
61 Kids' support group
62 Thirst

DOWN

1 Ancient city of Cyprus
2 Access ways to major arteries
3 Not anyone's
4 Informal affection
5 ___ Ducommun, 1902 Peace Nobelist
6 Stuffy, in a way
7 Show decisiveness
8 Show dementedness
9 Counter
10 16 magazine profilee
11 Year in Ethelred the Unready's reign
12 Mexican packsaddle
13 Index
14 Fragrant resins
21 Outback denizen
24 Sans animation
26 Offbeat ordinal
28 Same: Prefix
30 Crops
32 Bisected fly
34 70's and 80's cause
37 Via the mouth
38 Capital of the Kazakh Soviet Republic
40 Professional
41 Waters down
42 Capital of Veracruz
44 Nurse a brewski
46 Communication devices
48 Dress with a flare
49 Event of 3/26/94
52 The going price?
53 Item in a roundup
56 Rendezvoused
58 Hold down, in a way

by Charles E. Gersch

ACROSS

1 "Fiddler" star
6 Dido
14 Prosper
15 Fliers, collectively
16 Site in the "Aeneid"
17 Polite intro
18 Johnny and the Moondogs, more familiarly
20 Locks
21 Union, e.g.: Abbr.
22 Stays in line
24 Old trains
26 Get an ___ effort
27 Alphabet trio
30 Some Wall Street firms
35 Army bigwig
36 About 2 million in the U.S.
37 W.W. II craft
38 "Elle et Lui" author
39 Whirlwinds
40 Spotted horse
42 The Mormons, initially
44 Curtain accessory
48 Breathe deeply
52 Slothful
54 New York island
55 Halloween hanging
56 Adjective for a trifle
57 Issue, as a verdict
58 Put together

DOWN

1 Another name for God
2 Church areas
3 Artist Mondrian
4 Amphitheater
5 Smooth, in phonetics
6 Telesthesia
7 University officials
8 Support
9 Staff
10 Favorable factors
11 Bristles
12 Lady of the knight
13 Regards
14 It's good to keep these on kids
19 "To the best of my information . . ."
23 Hobgoblin
25 Glide, in Glasgow
26 Art Deco artist
27 Texas-New Mexico range
28 "The Ten Commandments" extras
29 Informal women's attire
30 Warehouse container
31 Stationery item: Abbr.
32 Cowpoke's charge
33 2 ___ (double-teamed)
34 Mercedes models
40 Blanched
41 Vinegary prefix
43 Posted
44 Mrs. Addams affectionately
45 Start of a Durante title
46 Sagan's "The Dragons of ___"
47 Gutsy
49 West Point inits.
50 Part of a pipe
51 Normal start
53 Nashville-based cable service

14

by Bob Klahn

ACROSS

1 Millie, for one
8 Sites of many bars
15 Cookout sauce
16 Land "by the sea"
17 Printing
18 Couldn't resist
19 "Stage Door" actress
20 Literary monogram
22 Nancy Milford literary biography
23 Fictional newswoman
24 "The Dance of Life" author, 1923
26 Cartoonist Gross
27 "Music City Tonight" network
28 Julius, familiarly
30 Miss named?
31 Modern housing
33 Get at
35 Veranda refreshment
37 Impious
40 Spread
44 Curling target
45 Kahill Gibran's birthplace
47 First offender?
48 He wrote "To be loved, be lovable"
50 Toughness
51 Smudge
52 Actress Rosie
54 Literary monogram
55 "Atlantic City" director
56 Emphatic words
58 Jurgen Prochnow nail-biter of 1981
60 Free
61 Table centerpiece
62 Affectionate one, maybe
63 Less radioactive

DOWN

1 Hugger-muggery
2 Roles in "The Godfather"
3 Steadfast
4 Basketball's Thurmond et al.
5 "The doctor ___"
6 "Travels in Hyperreality" author
7 Like some friends
8 Cure
9 Pepin, e.g.
10 Lady in Meyerbeer's "L'Africaine"
11 "Days of Our Lives" town
12 Conservative
13 Christmas refuse
14 Drugs, perhaps

21 Work clothing
24 The Furies
25 "Merry Wives of Windsor" windbag
28 Bar companion
29 Main
32 Blue Cross offering
34 Y class
36 Expendable
37 Visionary
38 "I'll ___ the Same" ('32 tune)
39 She gets what's coming
41 One aspect of earthquake study
42 Old Nick
43 Struck out
46 Capra's "The ___ Tea of General Yen"

49 Stopping point
51 Native Israeli
53 George Burns buddy Harry Von ___
55 Very short time, for short
57 Map abbr.
59 Do Little work

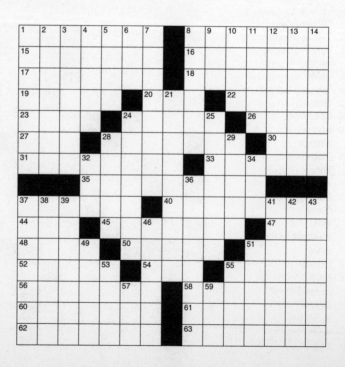

by Manny Nosowsky

ACROSS

1 Lab measurer
8 Divorce
15 Aid for dry hair
16 Prayers
17 Competitive one
18 "___ down!"
(phrase in car
ads)
19 Fine bit of
workmanship
21 Second X or O
22 This might make
you blush
24 Fool
25 Attached to
26 Kind of seaman
27 "Treasure Island"
prop
29 1919 Gershwin
tune
31 It's nothing at all
32 Court in
Washington
34 Put ___ to
35 Scam
37 Comic strip sound
40 Bobby's wife
41 Spot for three
men in a tub
44 Got misty
46 Long or short
amount
47 Flutter-kicked
48 Window support
49 Atlas abbr.
51 Believes
52 "So far ___ can
tell . . ."
53 Example of self-
indulgence
56 Unnatural
58 Electra's co-
conspirator
61 Passed
62 Its capital is
Hamilton
63 Mainz street

64 Imperative for
Dick and Jane

DOWN

1 Grand ___
(Evangeline's
home)
2 Golfer Woosnam
3 Controversial
canine
4 Make enemies
5 Macbeth's
honorific
6 Supply on old
spaceships
7 Words of reproach
8 First name in
skating
9 Print trials
10 Place for a tire
swing
11 Metric prefix

12 Survivor-take-all
plan
13 Fit for a doggy
bag
14 Eager, in slang
20 Fanta collectible
22 Headed
23 "Shogun" apparel
25 Wind down
27 It goes with apple
pie
28 Halévy's "L'___
Constantin"
30 To Frost it's
unloved
32 Fashionable
33 Boozy sailor's cry
35 Unkind remark
36 Self-enlightenment
37 Monopoly Place
38 Kind of blouse
39 Like plywood

41 Rid of dirt
42 Joey, for one
43 Wake-up times
45 Some
semiconductors.
47 Earth shaking
experiences
50 Edberg, e.g.
51 Jacques of song
53 Dog rewards
54 Mulcts
55 Math diagram
57 Media company
inits.
59 Tokyo, once
60 Took a load off

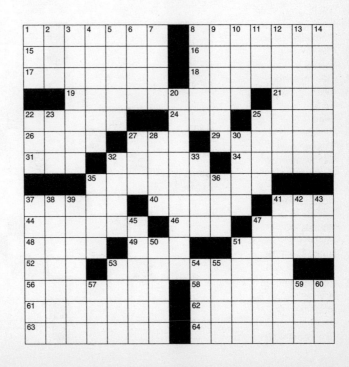

by Rand H. Burns

ACROSS

1 Mint or cumin
5 Not straight up
12 Culvert
13 Picnic shelters
14 Circus act
16 In quantity
17 Cohesive entity
18 Never, to Kant
19 Room extension
20 Baroque instrument
22 Squelched
24 The end for Captain Kidd
26 Bets
28 Head residents?
29 Kennel sound
30 The McCoys, e.g.
32 Tropical palms
34 Historic site of 1775
37 Lug
39 1969 Jerry Rubin book
40 Comedian Lehr
43 Old Chinese money of account
44 Neutral shade
46 Winning card, in bridge
48 Minds
50 Sibilate
52 Flabbergasts
53 Extinct apteryx
54 Award since 1956
56 Themes
58 Building material first made in Dorsetshire, England
61 He played TV's Poncherello
62 People gathered in a murder mystery
63 Brings back on
64 Pseudoesthetic

DOWN

1 Men of the hour
2 Jug
3 Counterculturist
4 Maternity item
5 Island group off Scotland
6 Diverse: Prefix
7 Radiates
8 Far out
9 Tweedledum and Tweedledee
10 Sambalike dance
11 Group in biblical history
12 Exemplary one
14 See 21-Down
15 Routine
16 Actress Rowlands
21 Asian capital, with 14-Down
23 Get ___ up
25 "Behold!"
27 Draped garment
31 Run
33 Some schoolwork
35 In a sick way
36 Suffix with right
37 Person in boots, perhaps
38 Site in a whistle-stop campaign
41 Vertical
42 "Swiss Family Robinson" author
45 Limoges and Sèvres
47 Sideboard supply
49 Kind of panel
51 Use a tiller
55 Directed
57 Drop
59 Three, up front
60 Kind of tea

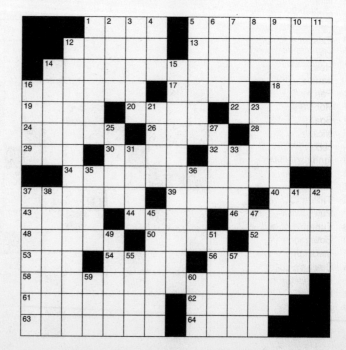

by Manny Nosowsky

ACROSS
1 Poor pad
6 Postpones
15 Rocket that launched the Gemini missions
16 Finally (and none too soon!)
17 ___ temps (meanwhile): Fr.
18 Unfinished business
19 Patently amazed
20 Fluff
21 "The Night of the Hunter" screenwriter
22 Just
23 Bryophytic
25 Cable TV choice
26 Cereal box abbr.
28 Sticking point, to Hamlet
30 Hijacker's currency
33 Pyramid builders
37 Existed naturally
38 Idle
40 Hester Prynne's daughter
41 Pantagruel creator
42 Roosted
44 Board of nails
45 Nickname in the N.B.A.
48 Ignore
50 It's a laugh
54 Ample scope
56 Trillionth: Prefix
57 Pull a scam
58 Turkey's home
60 Bother à la the media
61 Bourbon cutter
62 Raising goose bumps
63 Tables
64 Forest concealers in a saw

DOWN
1 Tick off
2 Swinger
3 It makes scents
4 Three-time Grammy-winning group with "The"
5 Banjo site
6 Like some ground
7 Reed blowers
8 Lake life
9 Maid, at times
10 Fr. holy one
11 Great Barrier Island
12 Score in a French game?
13 German naval base of W.W. II
14 VCR button
23 F.H.A. loan
24 Not as bright

27 Winter warmer
29 Hyper
30 Aware of what's new
31 Half and half?
32 ___ Na Na
34 Vote for
35 "___ was saying . . ."
36 Unhappy crowd sound
38 Bash
39 Follow
41 Chew out again
43 Odd-toed critters
45 Races, in a way
46 "Bye Bye Birdie" girl
47 Shared
49 Mount of laws
51 Lapis lazuli

52 Star of "Sun Valley Serenade"
53 Aconcagua region
55 Certain pubs.
57 "Good night, ___" (old TV sign-off)
59 "Cry ___ River"

by Randolph Ross

ACROSS

1 Beverage order
6 Entrust, as authority
12 Aches and pains
15 Emulates Romeo and Juliet
16 Fade away
17 Inattentive
18 Some pages
20 Kind of farmer
21 Mnemonic device
24 Quietly
29 ___ States
31 Jubilation
33 At hand
35 Cordage grass
36 Blessings in old Rome
38 Show distaste
39 Reasons for track meet do-overs
41 Medit. state
42 Author of "Murder in the White House"
44 Screenplays
52 DeMille's Delilah
53 Seriatim
54 Having a courtyard
55 Punctuates
56 Farm sound
57 Seconds: Abbr.

DOWN

1 1993 Kevin Kline movie
2 Carrier to 41-Across
3 Dandy's accouterment
4 Talented
5 Angles
6 Rod sites
7 Designer Schiaparelli
8 Campaign event
9 European auto
10 Matches
11 Paranormal ability
12 New York landmark, with "the"
13 Tercels and Prizms, e.g.
14 Subject of the 17th Amendment
19 Solicitation
21 Biblical spy
22 "When you wish ___ . . ."
23 Provided with a curved joint, in architecture
25 C.E.O.'s and B.M.O.C.'s
26 Muscateer?
27 Astronomical discovery of 1801
28 Computer command
29 Toxic compound, for short
30 Digital displays
32 Mountain climber's challenge
34 How sore losers lose
37 Breathers
40 Colleague of Ruth and Clarence
43 Rump: Lat.
44 Subject of anxiety?
45 Ahab's father
46 Narcissistic
47 Subject of Gary Sick's "All Fall Down"
48 Founding New Yorker editor
49 "y" to the max
50 Certain addition column
51 Radical 60's grp.
52 Cops

19

by Manny Nosowsky

ACROSS

1 Kind of stick
5 Guadalajara is its capital
12 Contract winner in the paper
13 Whom tax evaders fear
14 Typical introduction?
15 Wiseacres
16 Red ___ (sushi fish)
17 Man's hat
19 Chou En ___
20 Name in two constellations
22 Less of a risk
23 Apportion
24 "___ In Love" (1973 movie)
26 Alien cover?
27 Kind of order
28 Definitely not a petite
31 Made a loser a winner
34 "Enough with your jokes!"
36 Three in 5-across
38 ___ U.S. Pat. Off.
39 Nile valley area
40 It's of alimentary importance
41 Branch of biology
43 Figuring
44 Follower of fresh or foul
45 Authorized, in a way
47 Moreover
48 "No kidding!"
50 Fiesta brava participant
52 Gets extra shut-eye
53 Civil rights leader from Mississippi
54 Sawbuck
55 Presidential candidate of yore

DOWN

1 Famous TV liar
2 Start of the Lord's Prayer
3 Arthur Murray teaching
4 Scares off
5 Got overeager
6 Part of Will Rogers's real name
7 Foreign-exchange listing
8 Initials in tele-communications
9 Dirty
10 Build
11 Actor Davis
12 Bright at night
13 Overdo the wish list
14 Check records?
18 The Metro
21 Penalized in court
23 Relative of a cover charge
25 Lab burners
27 Cause to attack
29 Egg warmer?
30 Common Market abbr.
32 Wranglers
33 Galley workers
35 Gulliver brute
36 Muss up
37 Reprobate
40 Impose (upon)
41 1969 Hoffman role
42 Located
45 Creator of the Shmoos
46 Bight
49 Stag attendees
51 Johnny ___

20

by Randolph Ross

ACROSS

1 Reserve supply
11 Toulon's department
14 Grilled cheese go-with
15 K-6
17 It's nothing personal
18 Punjab potentate
19 Swore
20 Sapience
22 Mrs. Smith's wares
23 Hindu honorifics
25 Name at the 1976 Olympics
26 Hosp. area
27 Stretchy stuff
29 Hazardous boating area
34 Kind of fir
35 Mimic
36 Stooge
37 Alcohol solvent
39 Muse whose symbol is a flute
43 Perfumed
45 J.F.K. info
46 Duvall's "Godfather" role
47 Perot's Electronic ___ Systems
50 Secluded spot
51 Code of silence
53 Break up
55 "Shadowland" singer
56 Some bills
58 Bones
59 Setup
60 One of Fred's partners
61 Rated writing

DOWN

1 Prepare for takeoff
2 Virgil's writings
3 Dabbler
4 Breathing sounds
5 Times when écoles are not In session
6 Foreign assignments
7 Michaelmas daisy
8 Rock tour employee
9 "King ___" (1978 pop hit)
10 Blow one's top
11 All-purpose
12 Best-selling video of 1993
13 Celebrate
16 ___ boy
21 The cool place to be
24 Schedule
28 Montreal Expos manager
30 Came up again
31 45° sector
32 "Know ___?"
33 Chockablock
37 Biblical language
38 Persuasiveness
40 Court activities?
41 Stop
42 English poet Dowson and others
43 "Get ___ of yourself!"
44 Midshipmen rivals
48 Pageant prop
49 Check out
50 Early "Tonight Show" regular
52 To ___ (just right)
54 School district C.E.O.
57 Infirmary attendants, for short

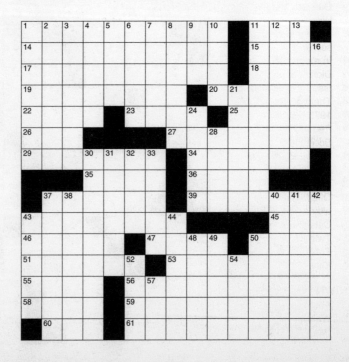

21

by Rand H. Burns

ACROSS

1 It's not yet due
4 Near the taffrail
7 Agitator, for short
10 Bartender's supply
14 Poirot used them to solve mysteries
16 Public house mainstay
17 "Artie" author
18 Supportive of
19 Familiar solution?
20 Ending of many plant names
22 Apollo 11's LEM
24 Complègne's river
25 Rupture
27 Lob
28 Rootstock used in tapioca: Var.
31 Conspicuous one
35 Radioactive ore
37 ___ "Che" Guevara
38 Wild
40 Boulliabalsae server
41 In medias ___
42 Dick or Jane
44 Issue
46 Thermoslike flask
47 1979 Village People hit
51 Eccentric
52 Dick
53 Fraternity letters
55 Place for a plug
56 Offering at the altar
60 Catamounts
61 Twisted
62 Trail
63 Kitty

DOWN

1 Absolute
2 Weirdo
3 "Man ___ Mancha"
4 It's at one end of the Dardanelles
5 Yalta participant
6 Shoe reinforcement
7 Racketeering statute, for short
8 Penultimate day
9 Jingoistic
10 Titan's locale
11 Unite
12 Crwth or kithara
13 Stone and Stallone
14 It's on the books
15 Holy ___
21 Acknowledged
23 Troops
24 Hospital employee
26 Iniquities
27 Quash
28 Blackguard
29 Remain extant
30 Untouchable
32 Through street
33 Chief Ouray, e.g.
34 Shipping quantity
36 Extraordinary
39 Boar's mate
43 Crescive
44 Kin of a 911 call
45 Red-clad cheese
46 Handy
48 Destined (for)
49 Engine parts
50 Wall Street wheeler-dealer
52 Minuscule
54 Marina space
57 Sci fi play of 1923
58 George Bush once headed it
59 Brit's closet

by Manny Nosowksy

ACROSS
1 Build-up
7 Literally, soft technique
14 Cheyenne ally of old
15 Extremely important
16 Inflammation of the respiratory tract
17 In a silly fashion
18 Boomer
19 Garcia Márquez's "___ Writes to the Colonel"
21 James and Clark
22 Business start
24 Young boxer, e.g.
26 Goes downhill
27 Classic name in mail order
29 He can hardly give a hoot
31 Compass dir.
32 Rush
34 Actions
36 Pictorial
38 Secondary listing
41 "Ready ___ . . ."
44 Agcy. that monitors smoking hazards
45 Dr. Zhivago and others
47 Vaccine name
49 To be, to Henri
51 12-point types
53 Old columnist Maxwell
54 Kind of gun
56 Unabridged editions
58 Something to believe in
59 Old profs
61 Curt
63 Pensioner

64 First and Second places?
65 Prizes
66 Fixes

DOWN
1 Old homesteads
2 Dive
3 ___ Locka, Fla
4 Counsel, perhaps
5 Chuck
6 Comment from Santa
7 Glyptologist
8 ___ tree
9 Athletic sort
10 30's Interior Secretary
11 Paris art treasure, with "The"
12 Soup go with

13 Book set entirely on the date 6/16/04
14 Pretend to be
20 Land of Enchantment
23 Mideasterner
25 R.&B. singer Bryson
28 Poker-faced
30 Red foes
33 Become eventually
35 Arm parts
37 Facts ___
38 Start of a chewing out
39 Computers working-hours
40 Browning, originally
42 Biased

43 Cold comfort?
46 Deer with three-pointed antiers
48 Finger-points, when said twice
50 Odd
52 Put into play
55 Desperate
57 Petitioned
60 Pro ___
62 ___ Cat (winter vehicle)

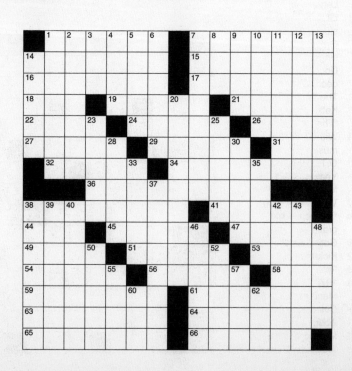

23

ACROSS

1 Market place
5 Frank
15 Fast time
16 Sophocles tragedy
17 Realm
18 Pioneering step
19 Law-enforcement support grp.
20 North Carolina school
21 Kind of journal
22 Gain a lap
23 Continuing subscriber
25 New Deal initials
26 "The Sultan of Sulu" writer
27 Frightened, in dialect
31 Jots
33 "The Scarlet Letter" topic
35 Lit __ (college study)
36 Gravel-voiced singer Mercer
38 Double-curved decoration
39 The Lone Ranger
41 Kafka novel, with "The"
42 Without varying, in music
43 O.T. book
45 Year Heisinki was founded
46 Verbatim
48 "Xanadu" rock group
49 Golf gimme
52 Kick back
53 "In"
54 1978 Barry Manilow hit
56 Customary extras: Abbr.
57 Made the circuit
58 Water trail

59 Highly maneuverable warships
60 Adamson heroine?

DOWN

1 Sight gags
2 "Friendly" dinosaurs
3 Singly
4 Bake sale grp., maybe
5 Thwarted
6 Wife of Paris
7 City at the foot of the Venetian Alps
8 Gradually slower, in mus.
9 Vindictive
10 Row
11 Org. of court players
12 Parched

13 Zola novel, with "Le"
14 River through Devon
20 Times
24 1977 Wimbledon winner
28 Noun-forming suffix
29 Providing strict order
30 Modern hairstyle
32 Tiny bit
33 Novelist Kobo __
34 Tsingtao vista
36 Ed of "Hill Street Blues"
37 Act as a lookout
40 Editing device
41 Hard to believe
43 Wrinkle remover
44 Caesar and others

47 Send
49 Mall carry-along
50 Sacred bull
51 Utter breathlessly
54 1961 Heston role
55 Serenade the moon
56 Farm femme

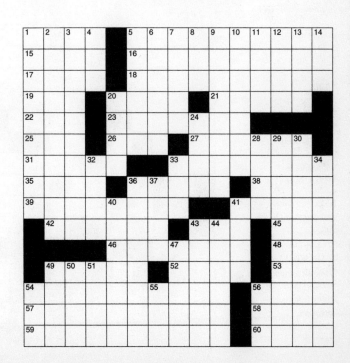

by Bryant White

ACROSS

1 Foretell
5 Recipe ingredient
14 Greedy, in Grenoble
16 Backward: Fr.
17 Carpenter's aid
18 Exiles
19 Oil containers
20 Child's measures: Abbr.
21 Do
22 Poet ___ Wheeler Wilcox
23 Dress necklines
24 Gridiron positions: Abbr.
25 Scold
26 District in Arabia
28 Rock musician ___ Vicious
30 Name in detective fiction
34 "Naked Gun" hero
35 ___ of troubles (beset on all sides)
38 Short race
41 Use cross hairs
42 1980's TV police comedy
43 Hold up
44 Postgraduate science deg.
46 Comic Gilliam and namesakes
48 "The Godfather" figure
49 "Mazel ___!"
50 Venetian blind component
51 Tropical ray
52 Fig marigolds
55 Deposit in a tomb
56 Wicked one
57 Color television inventor
58 Bowler merchants
59 Damsel

DOWN

1 Nonsense
2 Surmounted, as with gold
3 Stool pigeon
4 Swelling
5 Part of Santa's team
6 What Bush served
7 Like crocodile tears
8 Trains, informally
9 Parts of joules
10 Songstress Zadora
11 Firecracker
12 Uplift
13 Half and whole, e.g.
15 Discontinued trains
23 Article of food
26 Philatelist's need
27 Climb a pole
28 Sea dog's ropes
29 "___ boy!"
31 Utah town
32 Looks
33 Skeleton's head
36 Free-swimming worms with developed sense organs
37 Some parents
39 Say again
40 Instrument panels
41 Quickly, to a grammarian
44 Line of poetry
45 Hot beverage
46 Haphazardly
47 "La Plume de Ma ___"
48 Waterway
50 Put-down
51 Kid's marble
53 Early starter
54 Promgoers: Abbr.

by Rand H. Burns

ACROSS

1 Babushkas
7 Jullet's cousin
13 MOMA artist
14 Sports car event
15 Wheeler dealer type
18 Finsteraarhorn, for one
19 Material used in making insulation
20 Kind of testing
21 Hoofbeat
23 Disaccustoms
24 Year in Etheired the Unready's reign
25 Sub
26 Battle song
27 Draw toward evening
28 Thing
30 Willful liars
32 Clean, with force
34 Like possums and squirrels
37 Chico's partner
41 Aquatic birds
42 Chief Justice in the 1920's
44 Zsa Zsa Gabor's real given name
45 Little pieces of France
46 Groove holding a gem in place
47 He played Ponch on "CHiPs"
48 Grassland
49 Expunged
51 Winner at Chancellorsville
52 Prey of 15-Across
55 Colanders
56 Stage direction
57 "Communist Manifesto" co-author

58 Part of Egypt's boundary

DOWN

1 Bulging
2 Mustang's shelter
3 Noted name in abstract sculpture
4 Letters from Greece
5 City on the Maumee River
6 Assassin
7 Ship timber peg
8 Fabrications
9 Slate-colored, in Scotland
10 Heavyweight poet
11 Explosive made of picric acid
12 More wee
15 Secrete

16 Daniel Boone, for one
17 Soakers
22 Contaminates
24 Mediterranean language
27 Guitarist Phil
29 Gobs
31 No shrinking violet, she
33 Alone
34 Inclined
35 Unhand
36 Watergate, for starters
38 Film star's autobiography, 1990
39 Shorter version of 26-Across
40 Some sportswear
43 Chain

46 Cut obliquely
49 Went headlong
50 1856 Stowe novel
53 Brain wave readout, for short
54 Astronaut Grissom

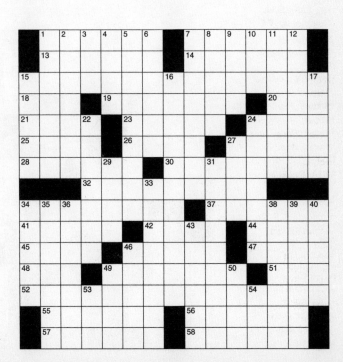

by Charles E. Gersch

ACROSS

1 Leaves in a huff
10 Calendar abbr.
13 Warning for the inattentive
15 Actress Maryam
16 Some fast-food offerings
17 "___ do you good!"
18 Prefix with benzene
19 ___ de veau (sweetbread)
20 Outcome
22 Rain check
24 Designation
27 Frigidaire rival
28 Matriculate
30 ". . . ___ to breathe free" (Statue of Liberty Inscription)
32 Ropes
34 Herders' sticks
35 Commercially O.K.
37 Pair
41 ". . . ___ a good night!"
43 Armenia's capital: Var.
44 Shows glee
47 About
48 Noted "Porgy and Bess" soprano
49 Sound
51 Actor David of "Rhoda"
52 Hoodwink
54 Rock's ___ Rose
56 Actor Gulager
57 Kon ___
58 More fast-food offerings
62 Dripping wet
63 Keep going
64 Albanian coin
65 Inexpensive telegram, once

DOWN

1 Woollies
2 Country since 1964
3 1881 fight site
4 Pre-show show: Abbr.
5 ___ Woods (California tourist site)
6 Bowler's problem
7 "The Plough and the Stars" playwright
8 It goes in one era and out the other
9 Ala. neighbor
10 Prophet who reprimanded David
11 Rectangular
12 Pioneer physicist Alessandro
14 Baton Rouge coll.
15 Letting go
21 Curious one
23 Crisp
25 Polit. label.
26 Business hub
29 Hard hat
31 Poet laureate Nicholas
33 Part of a blind
36 Office workstations, maybe
38 Winter wear
39 Legendary Spanish matador
40 Cheerleader, in a way
42 Actress Thompson
44 Popular vacation trip
45 Name in Western lore
46 Rather fashionable
48 Labellum
50 Remove
53 Answer to "How did you know?"
55 Hydro- or electro-follower
59 Organized
60 ". . . man ___ mouse?"
61 Project

27

by Gerald R. Ferguson

ACROSS

1 Stalwart
7 Pinning on
14 Hôtel ___ (city hall)
15 Serf
16 Kind of market
17 Intimate
18 Site of ancient Tyre
19 Gumption
21 "La ___ des Nymphes" (Corot painting)
22 Efficiency symbols, in physics
24 Suite
26 Pitter-patter, perhaps
27 "Rehearsal of a Ballet" painter
29 Runs rampant
31 Word from Beaver Cleaver
32 Area around the mouth
34 Shakespeare's ___ of Rousillon
36 Last-place finisher
38 Wooer of Isolde
41 A raiser of rye?
44 Secretariat jockey Turcotte
45 Left Bank body
47 Spook
49 Popular science magazine
51 Homes for farrows
53 Month after Av
54 Sewer connections
56 Composer Barraine and others
58 Randy's ice partner
59 Stickum
61 Decorative studs

63 Self-contained
64 Governmental pact
65 Gets cozy
66 Troops' stopping points

DOWN

1 Seeming
2 Not young enough
3 Coffer
4 Light-cavalry lancer
5 More cunning
6 Intolerable imp
7 Seldom-seen occurrence
8 You can't stand for this
9 Opening letters
10 Grinder
11 Period of antiquity

12 Loch monsters
13 "Brighton Rock" writer and others
14 Injected, maybe
20 Modern messages
23 Gobs
25 Review
28 Sports page listings
30 Old blades
33 Rivers in England and France
35 Harness strap
37 Spelunking equipment
38 Enter noisily
39 Salad ingredient
40 Diamond units
42 Chowder go-with
43 Little skippers
46 Exam taker
48 Beethoven girl

50 Not active
52 New Orleans player
55 Convertiplane
57 Stiff whisker
60 Wow
62 Kind of rally

ACROSS

1 Not quite tithes
10 Miles Archer's partner of fiction
15 Friml operetta of 1924
16 Advance rudely
17 Lifeless
18 Wide-eyed
19 Noncombatant group
20 Bust maker
21 ___ loss for words
22 Testifier
23 Greatest extent
27 Word with golf or grass
28 "Payment ___"
29 Broad-minded
32 Actor Morales
33 Plant bulbs
34 Southwestern Indians
36 1943 Agnes de Mille work
38 Palermo party
39 Some coll. tests
40 Outer layer
41 Germane
44 Try
45 Whips
46 Heliolater
51 Second cranial nerve
52 Singer born Clara Ann Fowler
53 Brag
54 Commemorating
55 Fairy tale figures
56 Stealthy

DOWN

1 William Drennan poem of 1795
2 Kind of wolf
3 Birthright seller
4 Air out
5 Mideast princedom
6 1969 Super Bowl M.V.P.
7 Skipping sounds
8 Slugs
9 Get the point
10 One in 100
11 Bourbon cutter
12 "___ With Me" (old hymn)
13 Antiwar group
14 Rose holders, maybe
20 Midway sights
22 Role for Elizabeth Perkins
23 It's usually white when it's little
24 Bygone motoring brand
25 Minn. neighbor
26 Bourbon cutter?
27 Payoff for early birds
29 Sweetums
30 Tweed's thorn
31 Carry-along
33 Most ancient of Greek gods
35 Alto ___
37 Features
38 Sly
40 Pound measures?
41 Foregoing
42 Kind of cross
43 Block of rows toward the back
44 Flavor start
46 Healthy: It.
47 Auto import from Europe
48 Farm pointer?
49 Conceits
50 Arbiters of plays
52 Immobilize

29

by Daniel R. Stark

ACROSS

1 Kind of bone
10 Movie memento
14 Turned off
15 When repeated, comforting comment
16 Summer Olympics event
17 Towns
18 Underwater peak
19 Buddha sat under it
20 Dug in
21 Match
22 "Melrose Place" role
26 Flatten
27 Ice and dice
28 Merry-go-round goal
32 Is green around the gills
33 Up
34 Economic success
35 Most elegant
37 Unexpected movement
38 Gets a check
39 Urban bombardier
40 Relieved
43 Catch some rays
44 Passionate plus
45 Candy store offering
50 Cover with strings
51 Kennedy alternative
52 Fine porcelain
53 Peps up
54 Sound
55 Grammatical concern

DOWN

1 Bird calls
2 Wings
3 Girl in a Beatles song
4 Burst (with)
5 Advances
6 Guliver's flying island
7 United
8 Moolah
9 Shogun's capital
10 One who's constantly snapping
11 One of les planètes
12 Presses
13 Hound
15 Govt. notes
19 Swagger
21 Know-how
22 Educ. establishment
23 Mrs. of TV and film
24 Efficient
25 Pie or pudding type
26 Shipping quantity
28 Integrate
29 "The Last Days of Pompeii" heroine
30 Canceled
31 James Cagney thriller
33 Exposed
36 Kind of solution
37 Totem pole's story
39 Matching set of jewels
40 Treasure trove
41 1970 film "Where's ___?"
42 Actor Flynn
43 Clemson mascot
45 "White ___"
46 Hat or teacup part
47 Cooper's tool
48 Legal restriction
49 Be steadfast
51 Shepherd's locale

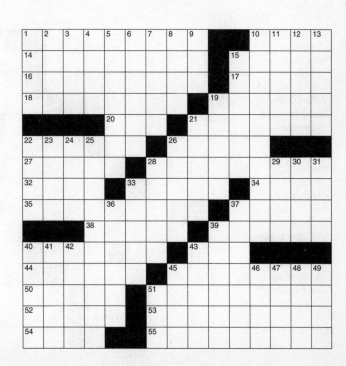

by Randolph Ross

ACROSS

1 Siegfried Line of 1930's Germany
9 Lashes
14 Cherub
15 Gym activity
16 Like an uninhabited preserve
17 Colorful fish
18 ___ time
19 Teen idol
20 Talk incessantly
21 Name
22 Olympics gymnast's goals
23 Clear sky
24 Jesus was one
26 Tim of "WKRP in Cincinnati"
27 Woodworking tools
28 Nine-digit ID: Abbr.
29 Shut up by force
30 ___ Maria
33 Turns gray
35 Pith helmet
36 At one's wits' end
37 Kitchen utensil
38 Graceland name
39 ___ Lingus
40 Liberator of Scotland
41 Counts
43 Bind up
44 Detached
45 Yeast enzymes
47 To-dos
48 1969 rock concert site chronicled in "Gimme Shelter"
49 Cube holders
50 Flight finishes

DOWN

1 Mule train drivers
2 Issues
3 What Hamlet sensed
4 Doctored
5 Commotion
6 On ___ (binging)
7 Mil. officers
8 Pop music's ___ Lobos
9 Fortune 500 abbr.
10 Upset
11 Is swayed by logic
12 Nuts
13 Causes of gray hair
15 A double, informally
19 At sea
21 Show stopper
24 Gets cozy
25 Far out
27 ___ Bay (New England site)
29 "Mrs." in dialect
31 Banker's point
32 Smog checks
34 Carrying on
35 Culpable
36 He reigned in Spain
37 Cold medicine
38 Imperative
40 Geom. figures
42 Clowns' shoe widths
45 Fictional dog
46 Pub drink

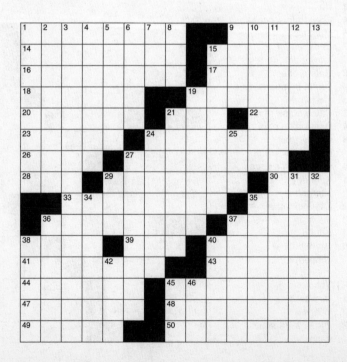

by Manny Nosowsky

ACROSS

1 Fuel source
8 Cracked
15 Serious lapse
16 Intended for those of means
17 Camerieri
18 Letter from St. Paul
19 Companions' separator
20 Missions of mercy
22 Breakfast company?
23 March time
25 Marked for exclusion
26 Study
27 Undercover agent, in slang
29 Carried out
30 Perscrutation
31 Old "Matter of Fact" columnist
33 Deserted
34 50's bash?
37 Back matter
38 Low bridge bid, informally
39 Extraordinary
40 Korean War flier
41 Dell turnover
45 Covered up
46 Welcome surprise
48 Lead-in for jail or pot
49 Slow down the mus.
50 Play mainly for defense
52 Northernmost city of ancient Palestine
53 It may hang by the neck
55 Kind of Emmy
57 Names, officially
58 Noble clothing once
59 Most temperate
60 Rappelling

DOWN

1 Arthurian knight
2 Mother in "The Glass Menagerie"
3 Duke of the old Dodgers
4 Fit of pique
5 Druggie
6 In a rut
7 Relayed
8 In a line
9 Hiked
10 Keb and Nut's daughter
11 AT's, XT's, etc.
12 "Ain't That a Shame" singer, 1955
13 Newswoman born in Bryan, Tex.
14 Clinton press secretary Myers
21 Place to be taken
24 Burned
26 Drag out
28 Anterior
30 Shoot at casually
32 Survey checkoff
33 See 44-Down
34 Big Apple V.I.P.
35 Doing recon
36 Without much to go on
39 Thigh-slapper
40 Shared by, to Shakespeare
42 First-aid kit item
43 Bee's target
44 With 33-Down, Presidential epithet
46 Some sacrificial offerings
47 It's a trap
50 Lonesome one
51 Aerobics habitats
54 Clear
56 Oddity

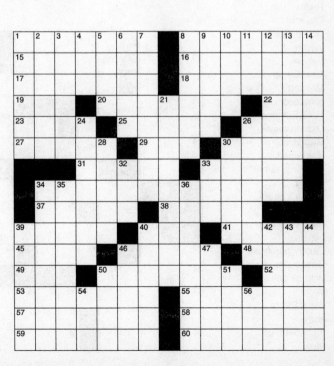

by Bryant White

ACROSS

1 Handel's "___, Galatea e Polifemo"
4 Pale purple
9 Stone: Lat.
14 Center square in a game
15 Architect Jones
16 Stand
17 Italian crowd?
18 Miss at the movies
20 Route near Bear Creek Pass
22 Trial
23 Lost enthusiasm
25 Limo figure, maybe
27 Papers for eds.
28 Shelter for troops
32 Actor Byrnes
33 Rivals
34 Thunder
35 This puzzle's theme
38 Service ___
39 "The Camp Meeting" composer
40 1949 Edmond O'Brien movie
43 Magnitude
47 Name part meaning "father"
49 Sweep
50 Archer's need
51 Physics topic
54 Fairy bluebird genus
55 Bakery purchases
60 Gaseous prefix
61 With all one's might
62 Black Bears' home
63 Alphabet trio
64 Slow
65 Massenet opera
66 Compass dir.

DOWN

1 State Department employee
2 Shipping unit
3 Freezing
4 Drew
5 Daughter of Cadmus
6 Historical Chinese name
7 Auden's "The ___ of Anxiety"
8 Reserved
9 Covert
10 Start of a children's rhyme
11 Soldiers of yore
12 Flashes
13 Hoaxes: Sl.
19 Hussein's queen
21 ET on TV
24 Flip one's lid?
25 Long-bladed hatchet
26 South Pacific island
29 Actress Davidovich
30 Hubbub
31 Orange blossom ingredient
35 Hosp. ward
36 Educ. group.
37 "It ___ Fair" (Sammy Kaye hit)
38 Arthur Curry's superhero identity
40 Some corners
41 Concord
42 Ancient goddess of fertility
44 Thunder
45 Hiver, e.g.
46 Sale item abbr.
47 Petrify
48 "Superfudge" author
52 Kabob thingamabob
53 Month: Prefix
56 Yankee Clipper's brother
57 Keogh plan relative
58 "___ Dieu!"
59 "Music for Airports" composer

33

by Gerald R. Ferguson

ACROSS

1 Certain sled riders
8 Gabber
15 Dish with toast
16 Played the chowhound
17 Spaghetti sauce seasoning
18 Quips
19 Friend of Theodore and Simon
20 D.C. insider
22 Diagonal spar
23 Slay
24 Practicer
26 A bit
27 It might need to be cleaned up
28 Informal phrase of endearment
30 Gunslinger Hardin
31 One ready to take a fall?
33 Felicity
35 Ad infinitum
36 Site of Jesus' first miracle
37 Brand outlet?
39 Puccini opera
43 Enclosure with a MS.
44 Filmdom's Brandon
46 It's east of the Atl.
47 Unionize
49 Legal papers
50 Held up
51 Attended
53 Thirst quencher
54 Blackbirds
55 As planned
57 Women's society
59 Intended
60 Constituent of DNA and RNA
61 "Where Angels Fear to Tread" novelist
62 Like shaked roofs

DOWN

1 New England speech feature
2 Gunwale feature
3 Pithiness
4 Get going
5 "Voice of Israel" author
6 Old Kobe coin
7 Drop in
8 Jo Anne of "Laugh-in"
9 Suffix with correct or collect
10 Captures
11 Fumbles
12 One-wheeled vehicles
13 Occasionally
14 Daring deeds of yesteryear
21 Nonpareil
24 Hung over
25 Actor who played Howard in "Melvin and Howard"
28 Experienced
29 They connect to carpi
32 Aberdeen's river
34 Writer Buruma
36 Quiet street
37 Friend of Antonio in "The Merchant of Venice"
38 Launch of 1962
39 Bound
40 Letter opener
41 Preliminary sketch
42 Done up in braids
43 Sever, in a way
45 More diluted
48 "The one that got away" and others
50 Woman's name meaning "lionlike"
52 Way with words
54 TV palomino
56 Passing mark
58 Pope's "___ on Solitude"

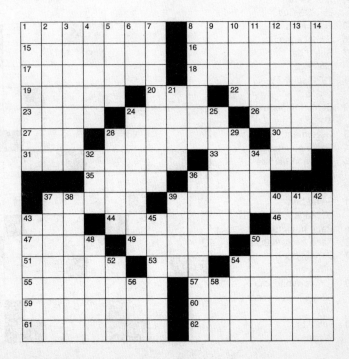

34

by Mark Diehl

ACROSS

1 Longtime first name in the Senate
6 F.D.R. had three
9 Tone-up center
12 Single-named nightclub star
13 See 7-Down
14 Sidetrack
15 Salad bar offerings
18 "Exodus" hero
19 Exam answer
20 Put into words
21 Covenant
23 Salad bar offerings
27 Billy Crystal, at times
29 9000, in "2001"
30 River transport
31 Mother of Hephaestus
33 Difficulties
36 Sweetie pie
37 Salad bar offerings
41 1972 sci-fi TV series
42 Some famous last words
43 Get-up-and-go
44 Apple purchases
46 Common Market money
48 Bridge unit
51 Salad bar offerings
55 Race track feature
56 Race track feature
57 Certain bond, informally
59 James Whitcomb Riley's "___ I Went Mad"
60 Salad bar offerings

64 "Here comes trouble!"
65 Flatten by pounding
66 Constellation next to Taurus
67 Hoodlum's heater
68 Punish publicly
69 "The Prince of Tides" co-star

DOWN

1 Tight situation
2 Aries
3 Salad bar offerings
4 Cortés quest
5 Blanc, for one
6 Salad bar offerings
7 With 13-Across, daily

8 Young salmon
9 Salad bar offerings
10 Groaner
11 Metric unit
13 Moolah
14 "Dynasty" actress
16 Tick off
17 Sole follower of song
22 Driving needs
24 Bit of mudslinging
25 Roger or Jessica Rabbit
26 Has control over
28 View from Ashtabula
32 Tidbit for the formicivorous
34 Literary pseudonym
35 Tallow source

37 Type of roast
38 Not in the area
39 Tommy gun?
40 Tropical starch
45 Bravado
47 Roadway maneuver
49 Site of many deals
50 Little: Ger.
52 Zip
53 Lay dormant
54 ___-cone
58 PC directory feature
60 Dog with a wrinkly face
61 "Gotcha!"
62 Pro choice?
63 ___-Magnon

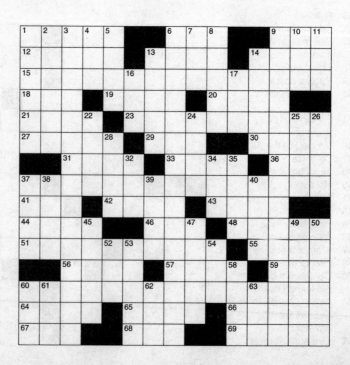

35

ACROSS

1 Sauce ingredient
12 Old spy novel grp.
15 Eden event
16 Trendy
17 Grew back
18 Verdi aria "___ tu"
19 Count, in a manner of speaking
20 S.A.T. takers
21 Police findings, for short
22 Lift giver
25 Arthur Miller's "All My ___"
27 Dear ones?
28 Golf-cartlike vehicles
30 Damask rose product
33 Pen brand
34 Main
36 Exchange for something precious
38 Deli order
41 Some woolens
42 Day's march
43 Indian name meaning "ruler"
44 Smart guy
47 H.S. requirements
48 In order
49 A few bucks
51 Pilot's heading
52 Philosopher ___ Yutang
53 Overseas pen pal?
56 Track components
58 Philippine native
59 Soap opera of 1954–74, with "The"
64 Its ZIP codes start 89-: Abbr.
65 Lucid
66 Describing some wines
67 Kind of sandwich

DOWN

1 Peak
2 Bank deposit
3 Onetime enemy plane
4 Song composer Milton
5 Off Broadway's "Tony n' ___ Wedding"
6 ___ customer
7 Raise a family
8 Like
9 Jets
10 Rank
11 QB targets
12 Track event
13 Piece of college jewelry
14 Ham companion
22 Summer resort south of Narragansett Pier
23 Scout out
24 Virginia creeper
26 Operated, in a way
27 Lily and rose, e.g.
29 Seasonal workers
31 Yes
32 Third man in a ring
35 Just out
37 It's stubbed
39 Narc's org.
40 Passbook info: Abbr.
45 Singer Peter
46 Carradine and others
50 VCR button
53 "The Apostle" novelist
54 Dramatic beginning
55 Specialist in 60-Down
57 Reward for merit
60 Modern music
61 Harem quarters
62 Ad ___
63 Year in Henry VII's reign

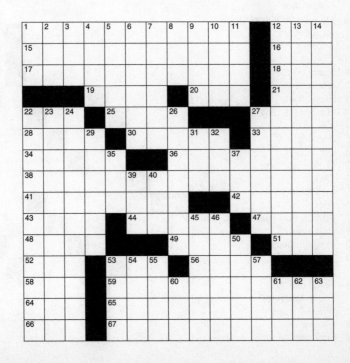

36

by Manny Nosowsky

ACROSS

1 Travelogue technique
10 Steady ___ goes
15 Owing
16 Ink dispenser
17 Sheet metal producer
18 Court activity
19 Pants preference
20 Has an egg
22 This señora
23 Minced oath of old
24 Legal matter
25 Radio-wave emitter
27 Extra costs in movie making
29 Trips
30 Hit ___ (aggravate a 57-Across)
31 Like Esau
32 French-Belgian border river
33 Do reporter's work for a certain tabloid?
35 Course average
38 Rusty on the diamond
39 Free again
41 Hassan II's land
44 X's
45 Properly
46 Set
47 Cartoonist Peter
48 Certain measurement: Abbr.
49 Popular dog name
51 Collimate
52 Museum piece
54 "Falcon Crest" actress
56 Ngaio Marsh's "___ a Murderer"
57 Where it hurts
58 Excuse
59 Sponsorship

DOWN

1 Unthinking
2 Development of an organism
3 Goes over again
4 It can be extra sharp
5 Sushi fare
6 Unit of electrical resistance
7 Summer dress fabrics
8 Fitzgerald and others
9 Bank
10 Balaam's beast
11 Kind of clean
12 From Geneve
13 Suggest
14 Awards since 1947

21 Stockpile, with "away"
24 Shows the court how the crime was done
26 Let out line
28 Complain
29 Basque "game"
31 Center piece
34 ___ warranto (legal proceeding)
35 Grace Kelly's middle name
36 Repaying
37 Strike a chord
38 More like mush
40 Pacific Coast critter
41 Sierra ___ (Mexican mountains)
42 Acclimatize

43 Bridge of 1590
44 Split, so to speak
46 Columbus's birthplace
50 It's a lock
51 Pick of the litter?
53 1951 Johnnie Ray hit
55 Meteorological prefix

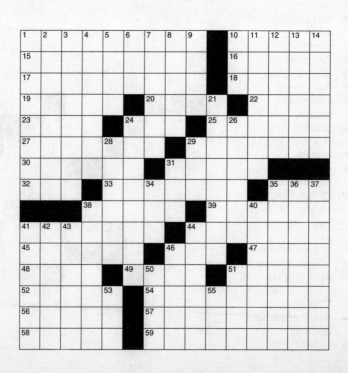

37

by Wayne Robert Williams

ACROSS

1 Plunder
7 Tangible tribute
15 Sweet-talk
16 Investigation subject
17 Picket fence
18 Disciple of Socrates
19 Agreeing (with)
20 Spica's location
21 So. state
22 Norton Sound city
23 100: Prefix
24 Go ga-ga
25 Old record label
26 Surroundings
27 ". . . the ___ are getting fat": "Beggar's Rhyme"
28 Referee's assistant
30 Word with street or buffet
31 Old World breed
36 Out of sight
37 Gone with the wind
38 Misses
41 Needles
42 Football positions: Abbr.
43 Saltwater lake
44 Counts' equivalents
45 Dreadful
46 Silly Caesar
47 Seed coats
48 "Paradise Lost" character
49 Not bought
51 Learned scholar
52 Takes up
53 Manifest
54 Forum honchos
55 Tried by fire

DOWN

1 Changes walls
2 Structural as opposed to functional
3 Trigger, for example
4 Ammonia derivative
5 Zilch
6 Physics unit
7 New World breed
8 Wields
9 Juicy fruit
10 Novel that begins with a mutiny
11 Final letters?
12 Suck up
13 Ancient region in Asia Minor
14 Delaware Indian
20 Miles and others
23 Sticky
24 Iron: Prefix
26 Actor John
27 Outfits
29 One of the Barrymores
30 Saturn's daughter
32 Money holders
33 Princess' pea, e.g.
34 On ramp
35 Took the wrong way
38 Machine loads
39 Jim Palmer, notably
40 Bedlamites
41 Commando
44 Lady with a lyre
45 Cup name
47 Part of conjugation practice
48 But
50 The "I Don't Care Girl" Tanguay
51 Implant

by Randolph Ross

ACROSS

1 Invasion group of 1964
11 "___ here"
15 River vehicle
16 Chick ending
17 Belafonte's trademark garb
18 Off
19 Father and son
20 1994 Shirley MacLaine role
21 Miler Steve
22 Z ___ zebra
24 Mean
26 Chesterfields
28 Ornery folks
30 Eur. nation
31 Absent
33 Alimony collectors
34 Sure things?
37 "Buenos ___"
38 With class
39 Leb. neighbor
40 Quechua speakers
41 Mountain transports
45 ABC news exec
47 Gallows
48 "Don't It Make My Brown Eyes Blue" singer
49 The Crimson Tide
53 Danube feeder
54 Dream states
55 Watson and Crick, for two
58 Kyrgyz mountains
59 1955 Anna Magnani film, with "The"
60 Where to go for the gold
61 Part of 1-Across

DOWN

1 "A Child's Christmas in Wales" poet
2 Slangy comment of optimism
3 Should it be that
4 Artist Shahn
5 While opener
6 Flu symptom
7 Speaker of baseball
8 Lawrence of Scandinavia
9 Newt
10 Peter, Paul and Mary: Abbr.
11 Mollifier
12 Obsession
13 Shows of good faith
14 Fits (in)
21 Fifth qtrs.
23 Tot protectors
24 ___ nails
25 More than encourages
27 Shakespeare's Sir Toby, e.g.
28 Monopoly card
29 ___ car
32 Chas. Addams character
33 Put out
34 1st Earl of Beaconsfield
35 Archeologist's study
36 A.B.A. member
37 Blueprint
40 Chemical suffix
42 Mexican War general Mariano
43 Coach
44 Security device
46 Noted spokescow
49 Anchorman?
50 Shake ___
51 Lorre role
52 Kin of khans
55 Chilly comment
56 Binary five
57 Chas. Addams character

by Manny Nosowsky

ACROSS

1 Relief provider since 1945
5 '48 Bob Hope spoof, with "The"
13 Cherbourg chow
14 Duncan and others
15 Bracelet array
16 Twice-baked bread
17 Title role for a Greek
18 Muslim call to prayer
19 X for Xenophon
20 "East of Eden" director
22 Noah's firstborn
23 Most immediate
24 Select, as a career
26 Kind of mail
27 English poet Hughes
29 Walpurgis, e.g.
30 Fast eddies' place
32 Cottonwood
36 Arena cry
37 Physical start
41 Revolt
42 Ohio college
44 Recite, with "off"
45 Lake transit
47 Feminizing suffix
48 Gull's perch
49 Bête ___
50 Upscale ski resort
53 Damon Runyon's birthplace
54 Grooming
55 Support for a plea
56 Incapable of issue
57 Rodin work, with "The"

DOWN

1 "Sweet" transport
2 Grounds for some fighters
3 New issue
4 Anne's double
5 Sliced food
6 Egyptian water barrier
7 Reposed
8 Palindromic Dutch city
9 it's often chained
10 Mythical maiden in a weaving contest
11 Official seals
12 Northern natives
13 Spiny, treelike cactus
15 From Pizen
18 Quetzalcoatl worshiper
21 Goggling
22 Blood brother, e.g.
24 Shady spot in the park
25 It goes around the middle
28 Schubert's "Grand ___"
30 Madison, for one: Abbr.
31 Foreign-exchange listing
32 Fanatics of a sort
33 Women's shoe style
34 Nursery resident
35 "___ Folks" (original name of "Peanuts")
37 Castanet player of minstrels
38 Thompson girl and namesakes
39 Papal headgear
40 Parts of pots
43 Verdi opus
45 Benji and others
46 Is syrupy
48 Be gullible
51 Requiring many candles
52 Budd. or Jud., e.g.
53 Hoods in hoods: Abbr.

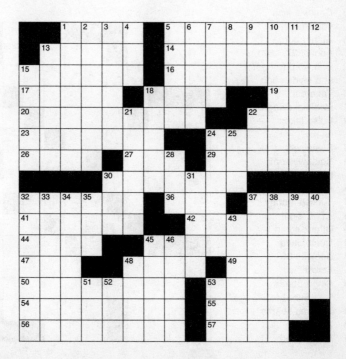

40

by Joy L. Wouk

ACROSS
1 Not straight
5 Plan
8 Operate
12 Ballerina Zorina
13 Share
15 Pierre's date
16 Book by 36-Across, with "An"
19 Russian whips
20 Families usually share them
21 Constantine the Great's birthplace
24 Samovars
25 Hole number?
26 Joined
28 Mister
29 Wad
32 Prospect
33 Fort Presque Isle site
35 Chuck-a-luck equipment
36 Author born August 27, 1871
39 Bad word to hear at a china shop
40 Take out
41 Habitual disagreer
42 Pulse takers, briefly
43 Sustained
44 Southwestern bandit
46 Kind of code
47 Turkish money
48 J.F.K. sight
49 Utter disdain
52 Dumbfound
54 Book by 36-Across
59 Ringo Starr's "__ Song"
60 Tapered seams
61 Irritate
62 Frog-kicked

63 "Kenilworth" woman
64 Alter

DOWN
1 Rock video award
2 "Solaris" author
3 Hematite, e.g.
4 Common
5 Coins
6 It relates the conversion of St. Paul
7 __ cent
8 Hazard
9 1976 horror hit, with "The"
10 Heckle
11 Passe-partouts
13 XX
14 Cleaned
17 Habituated
18 Petri dish contents
21 Adviser of the Greeks at Troy
22 Korean War invasion site
23 Brews
25 Bridge support
27 Grandson of Adam
28 Secondary attraction
29 Contrivances
30 Thalassographers' topics
31 Sotheby Parke __ (auction house, formerly)
34 Electrical unit
35 Christian of note
37 Baltic feeder
38 The ultimate

43 Gear for Sally Rand
45 Peloponnesian city
46 Kind of corn
47 It might carry coal to Newcastle
49 Without
50 Vittles
51 Lady Chaplin
52 Widest part
53 Colleen's home
55 Highest peak on Crete
56 Produced
57 "The Lion of God"
58 Besides

41

by *Randolph Ross*

ACROSS

1 Comparison maker
10 Rain check?
14 Monazite, e.g.
15 Plantation worker
16 Woolworth's, e.g.
17 High as ___
18 Suggestions
19 Free to attack
20 Turn black, then blue?
21 Date
22 Hanukkah dish
23 Sight at Dulles
24 Foldable furniture
26 Fusses
30 Most rundown
31 Cry of success
33 Gothic typeface: Var.
36 Spectacle
39 Like some motions
40 Feed bag morsel
42 Tart
43 Second of three X's
45 Magna ___
47 Spokes
48 Small chapels
50 Order
51 Jubilation
52 Lucky numero
53 Propagandist
54 Besmirches
55 Fall events

DOWN

1 Spirits
2 Least artful
3 ___ the teeth
4 Chary
5 Durango direction
6 Catarina's cat
7 Von Bulow portrayer, 1990
8 1990 remake of "The Texas Rangers"
9 "Men of honest report," in Acts
10 Sample
11 Somewhat
12 Second shots
13 Practice exam
15 Like Sinatra songs
25 Driver's needs
27 Precincts
28 Dental problem
29 Bandar ___ Begawan (Brunei's capital)
32 Structured like sodium chloride
33 Most meager
34 Pastoral land of ancient Greece
35 Comparatively poor
37 Prisoner taken 1/3/90
38 Gone
41 Samples
44 Dutch painter ___ Fabritius
45 Heating elements
46 Put the ___ (intimidate)
49 Repressed, with "on"

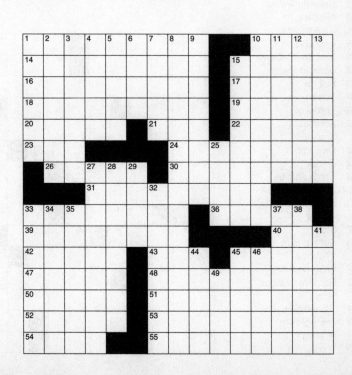

by Rand H. Burns

ACROSS

1 Some of the Dead Sea Scrolls
7 Guitarist Hendrix
11 Bygone cause
14 Way to Brooklyn or Broadway, in song
15 Breakdowns
17 Pithy depiction
19 Garnets
20 Mystery author Lathen et al.
21 Drive away
22 Brilliant conclusion
23 Fitness guru
25 Heed
26 Create a fragrant aura
28 The end, to some
29 Baseball Hall-of-Famer Combs
31 Crystal mineral
33 Miniplay
35 Bad-mouths
36 Faithless
40 Kiss, to 47-Down
42 Massed forces
43 Full up
46 Spirit
48 Throw off
49 Neighbor of Scorpius
50 Catch on
52 Chuck
53 Tomb articles
55 1955 Preakness and Belmont winner
57 Study
58 Apt medium for 17-Across
61 From now on
62 Remove blubber from
63 ___ judicata
64 Plant-growth retardant
65 Turned out

DOWN

1 Soprano Munsel et al.
2 Reading room
3 Girl in a Beatles song
4 Tubers
5 Thorax protector
6 Private
7 "The Travels of ___ McPheeters"
8 Nonborder regions
9 Tricky shot, on baize
10 Order
11 Job's forerunner
12 Take on more fuel
13 Not at sea
16 Sandburg's "___, the Dead Speak to Us"
18 Floor

23 Round coffeecake
24 Queen, to Juan Carlos
27 Quench
30 Churchill's successor in 1945
32 Craft with delta wings
34 Bowie the commish
37 Months of dawn-to-dusk fasting
38 Miss ___
39 Far out
41 Courtesan of ancient Attica
42 Disease, in combos
43 "She-Bop" singer, 1984
44 Check in
45 Flings of a sort

47 One who avoids "sissies"?
51 Matriculate
52 Little Iodine's creator
54 Dover or Hormuz: Abbr.
56 Defunct sports grp.
59 She was Glory in "Mad Dog and Glory"
60 Bus. mogul

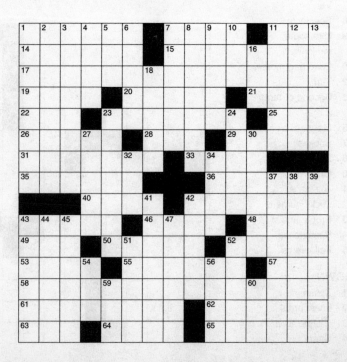

43

by Rich Norris

ACROSS

1 Shadowy
7 Throe
12 Informant
14 Brownish grays
16 Presumed
17 Female water spirit
18 Agronomists' studies
19 N.C.A.A.'s Cavaliers
21 Collect
22 Depression
23 Greenish blue
24 Scold
25 Mountain sign abbr.
26 Seating request
27 Summer abroad
28 Sporting org. with three million members
29 ___ jure (by operation of law)
31 Like Errol Flynn
33 80 winks?
37 Little, e.g.
38 Musical syllable
39 Ventured
40 Elysian abodes
43 Plane starter
45 Rap's Dr. ___
46 Allow the use of
47 Burden
48 Antipasto ingredient
50 Oldest city in Ohio
52 Friendly
53 Bring out
54 Benedict Arnold, for one
56 Fix, as a chair
57 Inducted, in a way
58 Norman Fell role in "Three's Company"
59 On cloud nine

DOWN

1 Snakes and lizards, taxonomically
2 Causes great resentment
3 Deli offerings
4 Spa features
5 Some Ivy Leaguers
6 Stimulate, with "up"
7 One who makes special deliveries?
8 Twinge
9 Try out
10 Echidna features
11 Like some jobs
12 Skewered
13 Theatrical event
15 Black Panthers leader
20 Poem that ends "I am the captain of my soul"
22 Egregious
25 River to Donegal Bay
26 Cinematic pooch
28 Tiny portions
30 Legal lead-in
32 Golfer's concern
34 Relinquish
35 Saturated
36 Made resolute
40 Gyrocompass inventor Sperry
41 Merchant
42 First name among tenors
44 Modern physics particle
47 Mink relative
48 Ending
49 Frothy
51 Der Spiegel article
52 Shade of blue
55 Chemical ending

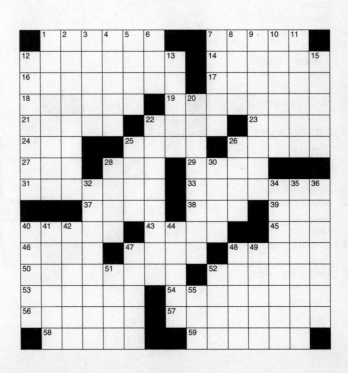

44

by Manny Nosowsky

ACROSS

1. Tops, with "the"
12. Sheep bleat
15. This is always out of time
16. "___ no use!"
17. Receiver of Niagara Falls
18. Price abbr.
19. Like "J" on a list
20. Yellow ribbon site
22. Dactylic
24. Carpentry projections
25. Elbows
28. Prefix with lineal
31. Weight
32. Ring yell
33. Smart
34. Corps
35. Le Gallienne and others
37. Silent greetings
38. Borgia in-law
39. Father
40. Baseball's LeFlore et al.
41. H+ or Ca++, e.g.
42. "Where's the profit ___?"
43. Best way to sing
45. Haul
46. Coleridge setting
48. Very, in Bonn
50. Preakness site
52. Geisel's pen name
55. Scheherazade hero
56. Certain sailing vessel
60. 1800's, e.g.: Abbr.
61. Rampages
62. "The Spanish Tragedy" playwright
63. Remnants

DOWN

1. 31st state: Abbr.
2. Med. school hurdle
3. Heist tally
4. Hounds' leads
5. Snap
6. City near Utrecht
7. Write a bit
8. Compendium material
9. Joan of art
10. Frederic Prokosch novel, with "The"
11. Sandburg's "___ and Steel"
12. Marshall Islands site
13. Electric signal diminisher
14. Rating
21. Popular investment
23. Polyester brand
25. Famous swing voter
26. "Blues Suite" choreographer
27. Be aware of
29. Use one's head
30. Salon supplies
36. Bristly
37. Complained
44. Rubber stamp
45. Castaway of fame
47. "Me, too!"
49. Rumored
51. Toward the mouth
53. Bowl over
54. Menu choice for E-mail
57. Occupational suffixes
58. That, in Tijuana
59. Map features: Abbr.

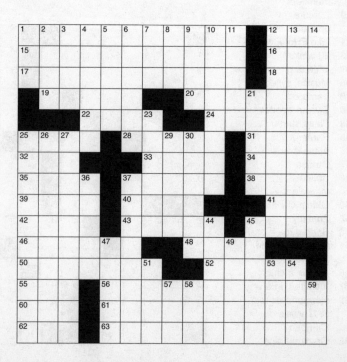

45 — *by Bob Klahn*

ACROSS
1 Full-length
6 Cubbyholes
11 Coati's coat, e.g.
13 Vile
15 Losing enthusiasm
17 Openly admit
19 Item in a surplice store?
20 Illuminated in a way
22 Forever and a day
23 Zest
25 Breed of red cattle
26 Caiman's cousin, for short
27 ___ for Peace (50's program)
29 Night of poetry
30 Black
31 Last leg
34 Old-fashioned country event
36 O.K.'d
38 Uniform hue?
41 No-win situation
42 Sleipnir, to Odin
44 "A Doll's House" heroine
45 Cambodian
47 Not out
48 Gaslight, for one
49 "Sweeney Todd" writer
51 Sample
52 Payload portion
54 Mew
56 Belgian airline
57 Coming from both sides
58 Stowe character
59 Out at the elbows

DOWN
1 New Jersey college founded in 1893
2 Stone relic
3 Philip Carey's handicap in Maugham's "Of Human Bondage"
4 Brief Egypt-Syria coalition
5 Crusoe's favorite expression?
6 Wait, to Spillane
7 Moses or Meese
8 Cling-on?
9 Dan McGrew's ladylove
10 Splendiferous
12 Geraint's ladylove
14 Seat
16 Arose
18 Some years back
21 Unfailingly
24 Baroness ___ Orczy ("The Scarlet Pimpernel" author)
26 Partnership, in slang
28 Turkish inn
30 Harbor haulers
32 It turns up at the end
33 Bozo's middle name?
35 Cherish
37 Polluted
38 Felt in one's bones
39 Round dances
40 Legendary landfall
43 Position strategically
45 Top Tatars
46 Actor Roger of "Cheers"
49 Have a bawl
50 "Phooey!"
53 One-third of TriStar Pictures
55 Capital of Germany

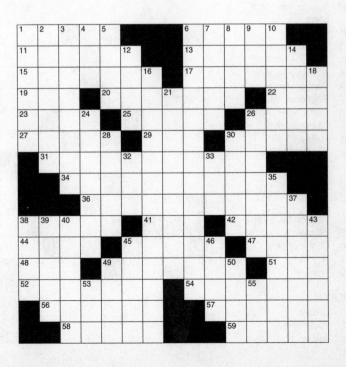

46

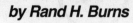
by Rand H. Burns

ACROSS

1 Cardinal
4 Sailed in a small boat
11 Sorted, as chicks
13 Toward the mouth
15 Spray
16 Resident of Asian Turkey
17 Perfumery resin
18 ___ vu
19 Headset, to hams
20 Rumpus
21 Itinerary word
23 Squirrel's cache
25 Salient points
27 Countertenor
28 Cézanne's "The Big Apples," e.g.
30 B.C. or N.B.
34 Cellular home
35 Pixyish
37 Returned to earth
39 "___ Si Bon" (old song hit)
41 Solid hit
43 Sophocles tragedy
45 In any way
46 Abrasive mineral
49 Dardanelles or Bosporus: Abbr.
50 Suffix with cardinal points
51 Ration
52 ___ Sabe (trusty scout)
54 Optional
56 Pittsburgh work area
58 Reason for a raise
59 Writhes
60 Castle of film
61 Razzed
62 Witness

DOWN

1 Lifelike
2 Widespread
3 Judge
4 Loudness measure
5 1944 Pacific battle site
6 Whole
7 Back
8 Taxpayer
9 Spa famous for its water
10 Favorites
11 Kind of turnip
12 Prattle
13 Art genre
14 E.R. personnel
22 Secluded place
24 Alley closing
26 Diminutive suffixes
27 Attach
29 Jittery
31 Atypical
32 Gift of Athena to mankind
33 Of civets, genets and mongooses
36 Brood
38 Like a cloverleaf
40 Whip
42 Upscale trio?
44 Stevenson hero
46 Boarded
47 Coeur d'___
48 Oswald the ___ (Chaucer character)
49 Transplants grass
51 U.S. Army medal
53 Onetime prime-time equine
55 Unversed signers
57 Grandson of Noah

by Randolph Ross

ACROSS

1 Cyclists' cousins
9 "Rambo" rescuees
13 Mundane
14 Scribes
16 Love songs: It.
17 Portuguese peso
18 Egyptian goddess
19 Head of a team of eight
21 TV comic Margaret
22 Words of Caesar
23 Island bird
24 Have it ___
26 Lighting specialists
28 Grain beards
30 Run ___
31 Pear product
32 Head garland
36 Suffix with stink
38 Breakfast food
39 Crime phrase
42 Special agents
43 Old Syria
44 Markers
45 "___ Man" (1967 hit)
46 Whirling dance
49 Without ___ (daringly)
50 Apt
51 Colorless, flammable gas
53 Hearths
54 After-dinner drink
55 Tarot reader
56 Consider in new light

DOWN

1 Robert Preston Broadway role
2 Wall Street unit
3 Kind of table
4 Split personalities?
5 Put on
6 LAX data
7 Thelma and John

8 Atomizers' contents
9 Click
10 Irregular
11 Charm
12 Car choices
14 Related to finances
15 It won't get far by running
20 Like ___ not
25 Worthy
26 Descendants of Moses' brother
27 Scotland's Monastery of ___
29 Punishes publicly
33 Overwhelm
34 Euclidean work
35 Endangered animals
37 Native Oklahoman

38 Underground conduit
39 Saps
40 Rowing equipment, in old parlance
41 Radio-wave emitter
43 King of the Huns
47 Chi. Cub or Atl. Brave, e.g.
48 By another way: Lat.
49 Top guns
52 Mag. edition

48

by Daniel R. Stark

ACROSS

1 Get juice from
5 Hunter's quest
14 Birch
16 Learned
17 Hollow rock
18 Glassed-in garden
19 Fortify
21 Boas
22 NASA robot
24 Put down, in slang
25 Livy's stars
27 Boil down
32 Modern outfits
36 Songwriter Cahn
37 Not a pretty fruit
38 "I don't believe it!"
40 Quiet spot
41 Brass
43 Stroke of good fortune?
45 "Paint Your Wagon" co-star Jean
47 Glove material
48 Curve
50 One way to the top
54 Ride the waves
59 You, evidently
60 S.E.C. employees
62 Ballerina Shearer
63 Alaskan waters
64 "Golf Begins at Forty" author
65 Zippy
66 Maroon's locale

DOWN

1 Stormed
2 Turgenev heroine
3 Ornament
4 Thoughtful
5 Maximal ending
6 Virtuosos
7 Fragment
8 X-rated, perhaps
9 Passes

10 "So ___" (Jimmy Dorsey hit)
11 Bedelia's home, in a folk song
12 Flood
13 Fitness centers
15 Niche
20 Try to mooch from
23 Temper
26 Greek "holy mountain"
28 Pasta dish
29 Novel of the South Seas
30 Slangy summons
31 Kid
32 Some crossword clues
33 "The African Queen" screenwriter

34 Strike monitoring agcy.
35 Roman goddess of health
39 Calendar rows
42 Going back to the start
44 Curry favor and crack a joke, e.g.
46 90's fashion look
49 High point
51 Creepers
52 Untamed
53 ___ secret
54 Nogales newborn
55 Slow movers
56 Brave
57 Norse giant
58 At liberty, in Munich
61 Pouch

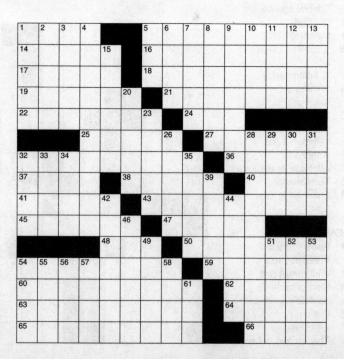

49 — by Frank A. Longo

ACROSS

1 Luminesced
10 Course
15 Fatalness
16 J. P. Donleavy novel
17 Kudos
18 Like many teacups
19 Ultimate
20 Tropical fruit tree
21 Split
22 Most newspapers
24 Plot
25 Sea eagles
26 Search party members
27 Backsliding
30 1981 Beatty-Keaton epic
31 Mountaineers
33 Canine cries
37 Hires too many employees
42 Spayed
44 Lofty nest: Var.
45 Snubbed
46 Bygone empress
48 City on the Bay of Bengal
49 Nectar flavor
50 Male cat
51 Nom de guerre
52 Chew
54 Shade
55 Linked in a series
56 Fired up
57 Vulgarity

DOWN

1 Throw dirt on
2 2.471 acres
3 Restless
4 Conductance unit
5 Feelings of discomfort
6 Cheer
7 Disneyland attractions
8 Parisian summers
9 Functional prefix
10 Absterges
11 Student
12 TV show's spot
13 Having protective wrapping
14 Dispirits
21 Brainteasers
23 Manannan's father, in myth
24 Stand in (for)
26 Aheap
28 Makes baskets
29 Made a copy on a floppy
32 Candle-wax compounds
33 Vivify
34 King's privileges
35 Financial support
36 Safekeeping
38 Burgh on the Firth of Clyde
39 Aircraft carrier escort
40 Sets that have limits
41 Ocean floors
43 Pencil topper
46 Seed coat
47 Overindulges
49 Famous name in TV talk
52 Year in King John's reign
53 Hoosegow

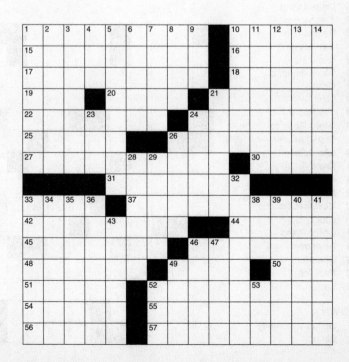

50

by Manny Nosowsky

ACROSS

1 Centennial year of old
4 Part of a Hawthorne signature
8 Food critic Greene
12 Rachel's older sister
13 Together, in music
14 Kind of belt
15 Phrase after "This is my final offer"
18 Inspired (very much so!)
19 ___ prof.
20 Remote
21 Bob Hoskins in "Hook"
22 Speed
25 Columbus sch.
27 Pearl Harbor ship of 1941
30 Does wrong
32 Treat too well
36 Begins campaigning
39 Eliminate
40 Ferris wheel cry
41 Coxae
42 Limit
44 Tidal bore
46 "Hard Road to Glory" writer
49 Like sashimi
51 Brute
54 Have a hobby
59 Be slightly nuts
60 New Mexico county
61 Bone: Prefix
62 Bowl over
63 Cheerful
64 Peel (off)
65 Lao ___

DOWN

1 Half of a comedy team
2 Solidifies
3 Overacts
4 A football conf.
5 "I now bid you a welcome ___": Artemus Ward
6 Relapse, with "a"
7 Andrew Wyeth's "The ___ Pictures"
8 Passes on
9 Crosswise to a ship
10 Establishment
11 Underworld river
12 Corp. name suffix
14 Lieutenant's insignia
16 "I can't believe ___ . . ."
17 Rain in Spain collector
23 Intersected
24 Ship, in poetry
26 Object of 60's protest: Abbr.
27 Multipurpose truck
28 Bluejacket
29 Indication of another name
31 Actor John of "Missing"
33 Caèn confirmation
34 Puck
35 They're groovy
37 Where the buoys are
38 Med. record
43 They get paid
45 Mideast weight
46 More than disdain
47 Former alliance
48 Allergic reaction
50 Tie
52 Is revolting
53 Come after
55 Principal principle
56 Physician's start
57 Water bearer?
58 Mil. officer

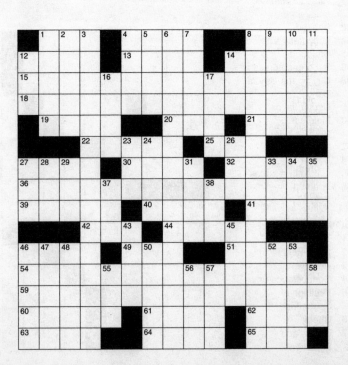

51

by Bryant White

ACROSS

1 Highlands tongue
5 Name of two former Supreme Court Justices
10 London's Old ___ theater
13 Maximum bet
15 Image: Prefix
16 Constellation near Pavo
17 Digital music maker, in old Rome?
19 War site, informally
20 Grand
21 Give ___ whirl
22 Suffix with depart
25 Germany's Tirpitz, for one: Abbr.
26 Irritant
29 Maison window
31 First duke of Normandy
32 100 centimes
34 Coral reef predators
35 Actress Ullmann, in old Rome?
37 Discard
40 Soft silk fabric used for linings
44 Actress Gillette
45 More bryophytic
46 Sailor, in British slang
49 Clinch
50 French marshal Michel
51 Election-night abbr.
52 7-Up alternative
54 Ingested
55 007's boss, in old Rome?
60 Cologne's loc.
61 Imaginative tales

62 Boris Godunov's daughter
63 Football Hall-of-Famer Healey et al.
64 Used an abacus
65 Ceraceous

DOWN

1 Tolkien's Legolas, e.g.
2 1947 Hope-Crosby destination
3 Dallas inst.
4 Healer at Valhalla
5 Soother
6 Elec. abbr.
7 Capone rival
8 Anoint, old-style
9 Staff
10 Kind of bean
11 With a temper

12 Mustangs race them
14 Overwrought
18 Hang glider's aid
22 "X-Files" phenomenon
23 Stimpy's buddy
24 67.5°
27 They're saved in trunks
28 Actress Liz
30 Exhausted
33 Pitcher Young et al.
34 Rare-book binding
36 Hungry
37 Storm
38 Approved
39 Nervousness
41 "Delta of Venus" author
42 Shoe width

43 Hold in judgment
47 Land ___
48 Political analyst's topic
53 Cigar tip
55 Wood sorrel
56 Put in stitches
57 Bibliographic suffix
58 Prohibit
59 1878 Kentucky Derby winner ___ Star

by Brett Blaylock

ACROSS

1 Logical thinker
6 Does laps
11 Scott Baio's "Happy Days" role
12 Least trusting
15 Reviewed with "up"
16 Agitated
17 Star seen late at night
19 "___ bien!" (all right!): Sp.
20 Tom Mix film
21 Kind of notation
24 Biblical measure
25 Helmet guardpiece
26 Sign
27 Nora portrayer in film
29 Makes rings in the hair
31 Joseph of ___ (follower of Jesus)
34 Snowmen?
36 Bit of snowman attire
40 Southwest Conf. team
41 Gift giver
43 Zeno's home
44 Where there's a lotta shakin' goin' on
46 Utter
47 Sandwich material
48 "Rhetoric" author
50 Wagner hero
53 Set off
54 Portuguese lady
55 Prepared for a wallop
56 Waif
57 Inflame

DOWN

1 "Eye" opener
2 1958 Literature Nobelist
3 Landscapist's color
4 "If I Could Turn Back Time" singer
5 Cruise companion
6 Playground equipment
7 Opposite of ruddy
8 Brit. adversary
9 Churl
10 Cast off
11 Smooth
13 Protests
14 Follow in another's footsteps?
15 Flowerage
18 Variety of gypsum
22 Price word
23 Muddy Waters's genre
28 Commence
30 Secretariat, e.g.
32 "___ Old Cowhand"
33 Chet Huntley, by birth
34 Furniture style
35 Appropriate
37 "Take ___" (order to a steno)
38 Swayed
39 Got along
40 Back-to-sch. times
42 Awn
45 Soft woolen fabric
46 Comedian Arnold
49 Sheppard and Turpin's gun
51 Gobbler
52 Mr. Onassis

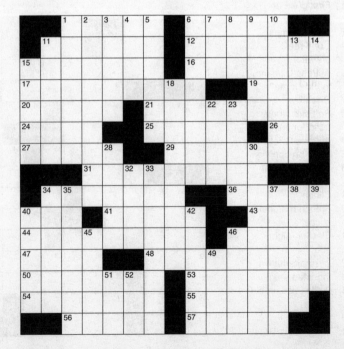

53

by Manny Nosowsky

ACROSS

1 Person not to mess with
10 ___ Barbara
15 Brown group
16 Rub off
17 Protactinium's atomic number
18 ___ Barbara
19 Gaelic "oh my!"
20 Conscious
22 Like some shampoos
25 Holy
26 Kind of pad
27 Scope
28 Scratchy
29 Bit of a charge
30 Firth of Clyde port
31 Bury
36 Catches
38 Toscanini and others
39 1985 World Series champs
40 Rep.
41 French entrée
42 Name of three popes
44 Part of Q.E.D.
45 ___ sting
48 "I Fall to Pieces" singer
49 Queer
50 Danger signal
52 Rock's Brian
53 Quinault's queen of Tyre
54 Disciplined
59 One of the Bowls
60 Tables
61 Person holding a string
62 Shock

DOWN

1 Storage place
2 Year in Nero's reign
3 Author Rand
4 Top film of 1963
5 Two-master
6 Indiana governor Evan
7 I
8 Crescent-shaped
9 High school student, informally
10 Movable place to eat
11 Sea into which the Arnu Darya flows
12 "___ Fighting Ships" (British annual)
13 Bony opening
14 Gains
21 Maintains
22 Grand Slammer of '62 and '69
23 Town on the Penobscot
24 Pulitzer winner for "The Optimist's Daughter"
25 "The ___ of Summer"
28 Tablet alternative
32 Ring adornment
33 "In ___?"
34 Kind of mouth or boat
35 It's rarely played
37 Signal that ends 50-Across
38 Bad fit?
40 Is of value, in a colloquialism
43 Club
45 ___ out (lose it)
46 Ruby's attorney
47 Dimwit
49 In-a-bottle alternative
51 Contemporary of 22-Down
52 Renamed oil co.
55 O.K. at sea
56 Go the wrong way
57 Palindromic city of puzzledom
58 "___ Ring des Nibelungen"

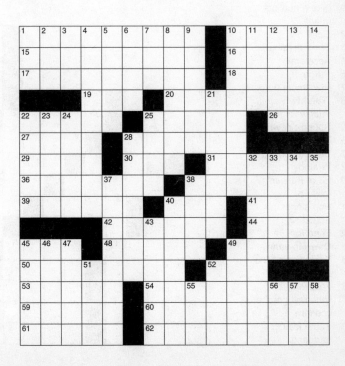

54 ————————————————————

by Rich Norris

ACROSS

1 Self-supporting
10 According to
15 Turnpike sites
16 40's jazz-style singer Ella Mae
17 Cut off
18 Prime
19 Greek letters
20 Pulitzer-winning critic Richard
21 Naval acronym
22 Profits
23 Look
25 Albergo offering
26 "___ Lover" (1959 hit)
29 Herd orphan
31 Toe preceder
32 Focus
34 Hindu divinity
35 Had
36 Checks
40 Like a nursing infant
42 Cask
43 Choir members
45 Accelerate
46 Purge
47 Blackmore heroine
49 "The Merry Widow" star, 1952
53 Support payers
55 Tend the plants
57 Sacred serpent
58 Wounds
60 Elf of Persian folklore
61 Pop singer Stansfield
62 Fend (off)
63 Down-to-earth
65 Trevanian's "The ___ Sanction"
66 Following
67 Cinematographer's concern
68 Some leather garments

DOWN

1 Patron
2 One in a flat
3 Possessions
4 Times spent on la plage
5 Ancient Roman spirit
6 Like a rainbow
7 In demand
8 Mashpee's peninsula
9 Ovarian product
10 Old-time actor Leon
11 Recitals, often
12 Type of medical care
13 Raise
14 Went over
24 Snake, for one
27 Response to a revelation
28 "The Last Judgment," e.g.
30 Studio prop
33 Word after "look out"
36 Highlights
37 Starry-eyed
38 Minor
39 Down to one's last nickel
41 Fed. agency estab. in 1933
44 Future resident, perhaps
48 Make bubbly
50 Curaçao quaff
51 Delegate
52 Staggers, with "out"
54 A natural
56 Asperity
59 Arid
61 Shenanigan
64 High school subj.

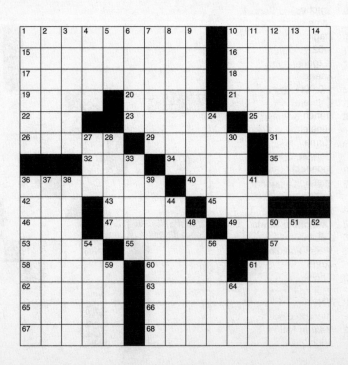

55

by Bryant White

ACROSS

1 Renounce
7 Half of sei
10 Pearl Mosque city
14 Lunch hour meeting, e.g.
15 Charles IX's successor
17 Pitchman
18 Outer
19 British ___
20 Sufferers of senility
21 Plover
23 Cocteau's "___ Enfants terribles"
24 Brit. award
27 Mountain road feature
28 French social philosopher Georges
31 Felt sun hat
33 Teachers' org.
34 Some drafts
35 Tragicomic play of 1952
40 Fitzgerald and others
41 100,000 rupees
42 In its entirety
43 French assembly
45 Constellation near Norma
48 Work steadily at
49 I opener?
51 Yeast
53 August birthstone
55 Wonderstruck, in a way
56 Etching process
59 Amatory
60 Sweet wine
61 Puccini opera
62 Author of "The Road Less Traveled"
63 Compass dir.
64 Thin

DOWN

1 Remedy
2 Increases
3 ___ law (physics principle)
4 ___ den Linden (Berlin boulevard)
5 Cup name
6 Be off the mark
7 On ___ (precisely)
8 Drugstore name
9 ___-temps (meanwhile): Fr.
10 Haughtiness
11 Singapore sling ingredient
12 Fjord's kin
13 Trouble
16 Algeria's flag has one
22 Anderson et al.
24 Fig Newton rival
25 "Contempt" star, 1963
26 Frozen Wasser
29 Half of a TV duo
30 25¢ picture
32 ___ and dart (molding design)
34 Certain train
35 Fountainhead
36 Conjoin
37 Common oath
38 Lustrous fabric
39 Noh prop
40 Shoot à la Buck Rogers
43 Foolish pranks
44 Shred
45 1975 Belmont Stakes winner
46 Fixes the donkey's tail
47 Short story
50 Coarsely ground hominy
52 Where drachmae changed hands
53 Stuff
54 Plug of half-smoked tobacco
56 Roadie's burden
57 Ici on parle français: Abbr.
58 Trojans' home
59 Unexpected visitors, for short

56

by Chuck Deodene

ACROSS

1 Conned
7 Toyota model
12 It's after Letterman, for many
13 Toulouse-Lautrec and others
14 Etched
15 Proud one
16 Drudge
17 Does the voice-over, perhaps
18 Star of the "Herbie" movies
22 Wedding vows
23 R.N.'s posting
24 Sun ___-sen
25 Sough
26 Stick
28 Pit
32 Prized feather source
33 Popular women's monthly
35 Artist's prefix
36 Not well-kept
38 Soaks up
39 Year in the reign of Justinian I
40 One of the Gyclades
42 Yellow, in a way
43 Mark: Lat.
44 Modern-day worry
47 Kudos
49 Tombstone brothers
50 Inconsistent
51 Sheet material
53 Destiny
54 Some coats
55 Impale
56 Opposed to, poetically

DOWN

1 Twins' arena
2 Political zealot
3 Is "ripe"
4 Dialogue
5 E.R. employee
6 ___ volente
7 Oft-adjusted items on planes
8 Boorish
9 Spur
10 "We, the People" playwright
11 Impetrates, with "for"
12 Stangy cause of unease
13 ___ Penny
15 Crusty one
19 Beguile
20 Stomach ___
21 PT 109, e.g.
26 Device for measuring extreme cold
27 Pig out
29 64,000 Europeans
30 Rare delivery?
31 Sugar byproduct
34 "From Here to Eternity" actor Philip
37 Miniature re-creation
41 Schism
43 Fresh-meat provision
44 Hex
45 O. J.'s alma mater
46 Worm: Prefix
47 Albanian coins
48 Doesn't give ___
51 Identify
52 Big Band, e.g.

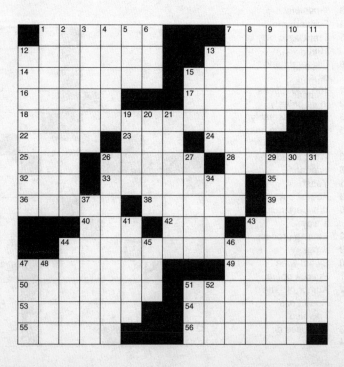

by John Stanley

ACROSS

1 Midwest Indian
5 One of the Seven Sages of ancient Greece
9 Sharpener
14 Item of earthenware
15 Yarn opener
16 Like elm leaves
17 Made a liar of
19 Arrest
20 Fisherman's gear
21 Continuing
23 Put in order
24 Running track material
25 Purposeful
26 Motorcycle hero
27 Kind of card
28 Yields
32 More saponaceous
37 Pulitzer-winning poet Gary et al.
38 Auto designer Maserati
39 Surplus
40 It's near Piccadilly Circus
41 Swinehulls
45 Split-up of 1970
48 Flirts
49 Large, sweet cherry
50 Rose
52 Left
53 Brain clutter
55 1934 Douglas Freeman biography
56 Eastern royalty
57 Mel and family
58 Goes downhill
59 Chair support
60 Gossip

DOWN

1 Covers some ground
2 Turnoff
3 Northern Irelander
4 Film director Jonathan
5 Pop music family of the 50's–70's
6 Coin
7 Close friend, in slang
8 Lotharios
9 On an even keel
10 Transported in wheelbarrows
11 Somewhat angular typeface
12 Basket material
13 Isn't finalized
18 Sacrifice, e.g.
22 "The Guns of Navarone" star
25 Smooth
29 Queen with a famous bust
30 Cuts across
31 Frequent fliers
33 Bugged
34 Leaves alone
35 Wild blue yonder
36 Strutters
41 Claremont, Calif., college
42 Fielder's cry
43 Stick
44 Master Schofield of fiction
45 Tusked animals
46 Throw out
47 Sinatra film "___ in the Head"
51 Break into bits
54 Pharmacist's compound

by Wayne Robert Williams

ACROSS

1 Camera settings
7 Reprobate
15 1970's Best Picture
16 "Shogun" rite
17 Secluded spot
18 Like Toons
19 Cedar Rapids college
20 Verdugo and others
22 Not share
23 Partake of
24 Work long and hard
25 Store, in a way
28 Air bubble
30 African sorceress of fiction
32 At the age of: Lat., abbr.
33 Agamemnon's father
36 Rocky ridge
38 1940 Hope film
43 Lissome
44 Stealth craft
45 Scratchy shrub
48 Chopper
50 ___ bene
51 Camels' kin
53 Furthermore
56 Prefix meaning failure
57 Roy Orbison's "___ Over"
58 Playwright Norman
60 Queen before Sophia
61 Refute
64 Personal spa
66 Dubai and others
67 Disentwine
68 Security
69 Hitchcock book "A ___ of a Different Color"

DOWN

1 Longest key
2 City north of Sunnyvale
3 And like that
4 Ike's arena
5 Peaceable types
6 New Zealand runner Peter
7 1932 Dietrich film
8 Miracle site
9 Greet the day
10 Flight
11 Police-blotter letters
12 Hip
13 Interstice on an insect's wing
14 Role for seven actresses
21 Sister of Selene
26 Durban's province
27 Enter gradually
29 Chaos
31 Directional ___ suffix
34 City on the Mohawk
35 Soak
37 Fellow, in slang
39 ___ Na Na
40 Part of a dash
41 Hangers-on
42 Penciled-in
45 Vacation mementos
46 Last syllable of a word
47 Backbone of a mountain range
49 1994 U.S. Open golf champ Ernie
52 Walloped
54 "Yup"
55 Rhone tributary
59 Ancient greetings
62 Before indicator
63 Tore
65 Singer's syllable

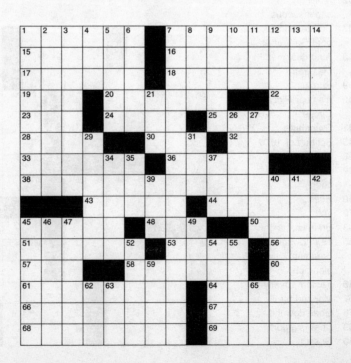

59

by Randolph Ross

ACROSS

1 Goldfinger's target
9 Chest on the Spanish Main
13 Egg order
14 Guarantee
16 Change of mind
17 Source of shoots
18 Meadowlands
19 Hoddy-doddies
20 Crewman
21 Ant, in dialect
23 Cellular prefix
24 Extract
28 Sore winner
30 Magician's secret place
31 Necessitated
32 The 8 in V-8
34 "Shh!"
37 Tomato troubles
41 Sisyphean
42 Opening word
43 Address abbr.
44 Represent in person
47 Little of Scotland
48 Yank in the Yucatán
50 Props and scenery
54 Police presentation
55 Put on one's thinking cap
56 Means of admittance
57 Mean person
58 Paris newspaper France-___
59 Sidewalk entrepreneurs

DOWN

1 Skips
2 In general
3 Mental vacation, so to speak
4 Clothes hanger
5 "Show Boat" composer
6 Endeavour initials
7 River to the Missouri
8 Plant circulatory system
9 Cutting-edge
10 Villa Borghese site
11 Like dice
12 Attendant
14 Election tippers, sometimes
15 Presided over
22 Care
25 Mr. Rhodes of Rhodesia
26 Eli, for one
27 Shorten
29 Surges
31 M.D. specialty
33 Think tank: Abbr.
34 Rob
35 Female hormones
36 Use X-ray vision
38 Rolfing
39 Current calculator
40 Ushers
45 Org. co-founded by Victor Herbert
46 Coal burner
49 Rodolfo ___ first Mexican astronaut
51 Hoary
52 Prepare for action
53 Library catalogue abbr.

by Rich Norris

ACROSS

1 Ruins
9 Sprees
14 Discuss in detail
15 Iced dessert
17 Develop slowly
18 "Wanted" poster, e.g.
19 Governmental
20 Reviewer of books, for short
22 Endorses
23 Shipping need
24 Offensive
27 Charge
28 Crunch maker
30 Jewelry item
32 Humerus neighbor
34 Takes it easy
35 Popular TV personality
40 Longtime New Yorker cartoonist Charles
41 Saskatchewan native
42 Aristocratic rule
45 Impose
49 Follow persistently
50 Family members
52 Scholarship factor
54 Followed closely
56 Musical ability
57 Wife of 31-Down
58 Frisco 11
60 Make the best of
63 Hush-hush
64 Exposed, with "out"
65 Actress Berger
66 Like a savanna

DOWN

1 Lamb essay "Mrs. Battle's Opinions on ___"
2 Banging noise
3 Reading pulp fiction, e.g.
4 Flumes
5 Honshu city
6 Marilu Henner's role on "Evening Shade"
7 Gain
8 Put up
9 Bridge holding
10 "Foucault's Pendulum" author
11 Some tabernacle singers
12 Picnic spoiler
13 Revolted
16 Starts the frame over in bowling
21 Food for junior
24 Associate
25 Addition column
26 Double crosses
29 Retire
31 Presidential monogram
33 Former nuclear power agcy.
35 Crates
36 Urgency
37 Applesauce
38 "Dies ___"
39 Agent Youngfellow's boss
40 Portable chairs
43 Catnap
44 "Knock ___ Kiss" (1942 hit)
46 Cloisonné feature
47 Phoenician, for one
48 Confiscates
51 Choral music composer William
53 1936 Cooper role
55 "After Dark, My Sweet" star
57 Entangle
59 Military name abbr.
61 By means of
62 Number of coins in the fountain

61

by Charles E. Gersch

ACROSS

1 Restoration monarch
10 Asian capital of 6.1 million, old-style
15 "Wheel of Fortune" space
16 Polonius's inadequate protection
17 Sheila Weller's 1993 biographee
18 Active ones
19 Algeria's Noureddine Morceli, e.g.
20 Exotic zoo animal
22 Saint ___, France
23 Having more than one: Abbr.
24 Shellac
25 Ex-tyrant
26 Together: Prefix
27 1945 meeting site
29 Bake sale group, perhaps
30 1901 Maugham novel, with "The"
31 Network component
33 Rise
36 Frank's friend in the comics
37 Smokey, once
39 Batter's ploy
40 Butt
41 Acknowledgment of error?
43 Stanley, e.g.
46 Wine pitcher
48 Authorizes
49 Phone intro
50 Football yardage
51 Aches
52 "So ___ I know"
53 In the vicinity of once
55 Items often reset

57 Fretful
58 Stymie
59 Rival of Helena
60 Like a variety of sheep

DOWN

1 Squeezers
2 Lesson
3 Safety
4 Use, as files, with "to"
5 Cozy hollow
6 Popular 80's dolls
7 Indonesian leader
8 Radio actress Rich et al.
9 Advances
10 Pater
11 Bakery attraction
12 Three Stooges prop

13 "___ Way" (Pacino film)
14 Vocally similar
21 Dabblers
24 Slacks material
27 What "d" stands for
28 W.W. I battle site
30 Part of H.R.H.
32 Cause of a blowup
33 Nullify
34 Places for knots
35 Most amusingly exaggerated
38 Contest on the range
39 Gets financial control of
42 First name on the Supreme Court
43 Life, for one

44 Peter Lorre's "Casablanca" role
45 Forwent
47 Related maternally
49 Prefix with lineal
52 White cheese
54 White alternative
56 Denver zone: Abbr.

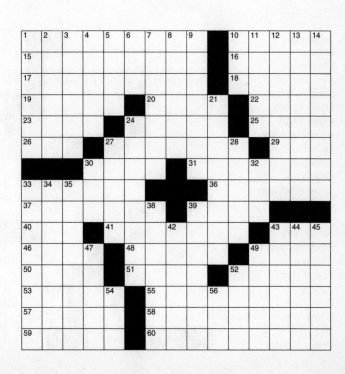

62

by Randolph Ross

ACROSS

1 Exaggerate
8 More than a dash: Abbr.
11 Shaky voices
13 Singers John and Bonnie
17 Cats' comments
18 Strip of paint
19 Prayer word
20 Palindrome part
21 Asian pipe
22 Prerevolutionary Russian commune
23 Started from scratch
25 Preparation for drilling?
26 Toward the Levant
28 One who's not in
30 Calendar mo.
31 Berth place
35 Prof.'s aides
36 Liars
38 Tampa Bay N.F.L.er
39 Waning
41 First word of Montana's motto
42 Narrow route
43 Cuisine type
44 It's overexacting
46 River through Lake of the Ozarks
50 Cockpit dial abbr.
51 Beyond the exurbs
52 ___ surgery
53 Advanced degree
54 Contrivances
56 "Old soldiers ___ . . ."
58 Stow cargo
59 Whiny one
60 Mint
61 Unity

DOWN

1 Monopoly property
2 Craze of 1983
3 Backtracks
4 Glasgow uncle
5 Carrier
6 Old-time cartoonist Briggs
7 Sank a putt
8 1989 Broadway monodrama
9 Ancient Jewish council
10 Embroidery loop
12 Alpine instruction
14 1960 Jayne Mansfield movie
15 Suffer battlefield losses
16 Twitches
24 Look
27 Ball holder
29 Asian cereal grass
32 Preteen romance
33 Impression
34 False
37 Friday on TV, e.g.: Abbr.
38 French villages
40 Levied congregants
45 Japanese soup
47 "There ___ ghosts, you say": Noyes
48 MacLeod of "The Mary Tyler Moore Show"
49 Professeur's charge
55 Hem, not haw
57 TV cartoon chihuahua

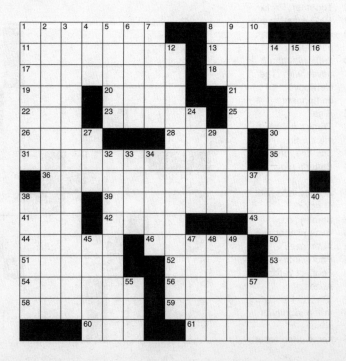

63

by Manny Nosowsky

ACROSS

1 Hyped shopping area
12 Where gains are registered?
14 Democratic
16 ___ high (elated)
17 Get the juices flowing
18 Haile Selassie worshiper
19 Folded food
22 Elevator stop: Fr.
24 Yon ship
25 Threadlike structure
26 See
27 Offensive
28 Ridges
30 Actress Berger
32 Denounce as a Communist
34 Tantrum thrower, perhaps
38 Kind of nerve
40 Straight man
41 Fishing boat
44 The East
46 Composer Bruckner
47 Cable TV's Emmy
48 Mouthed phrase from the bench
49 Lips
50 Philippine seaport
52 ___ League (group since 1945)
54 Ending with the most
55 Electricity pioneer
59 High-pressure springs
60 Music center

DOWN

1 Cuffed
2 Communications conglomerate
3 Fraternity letter
4 Knowledge
5 Covered
6 Nymphets
7 Abu Dhabi and Dubai
8 Denver zone: Abbr.
9 "See if ___"
10 1814 Byron poem
11 Old Testament miracle worker
12 Netherlands Antilles island
13 Downed
14 Near
15 British stoolie
20 Purchase more than
21 Feminist Eleanor
23 Ladies' men
27 1884 Helen Hunt Jackson romance

29 War zone of '67
31 Destroy
33 Hobart is its capital
35 Unwanted overhang
36 "My" kind of folks
37 Soprano Scotto
39 Mayor Richard of Los Angeles
41 Hugo Ball movement
42 Florida's ___ National Forest
43 Go back
45 ___ tablets (Egyptian cuneiform treasures)
48 Pants: Ger.
51 Barberi d'___ (Italian wine)

53 Fiesta or fish follower
56 Deadly biter
57 Speed: Abbr.
58 Roar from the crowd

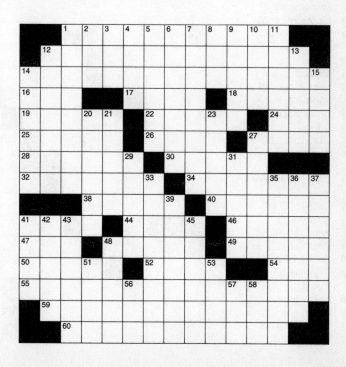

64

by Randolph Ross

ACROSS

1 Called
5 Pattern
13 Untamed
14 Helps get through
15 Spot ___
16 Burberrys
17 "What's the Frequency, Kenneth?" group
18 Part of a New England skyline
20 Site of many scrapes
21 Indonesia's ___ Islands
22 Actress Allgood et al.
23 Dearies
24 Alternatives to Rivieras
26 Sorry
27 Like an old schoolhouse
28 Big Apple couple
32 Run with quick, small steps
33 Ready
34 Mideast native
35 More in need of a brushoff?
36 Cedar Rapids college
37 Like
38 It needs renewal
40 Springe
41 Vietnamese New Year
42 Cruise
43 Sinatra's "___ Way"
44 Verdi aria "___ tu"
45 On the offensive
47 "I got the ___ the morning . . ."
49 Under control
50 Gush
51 Held, as claims
52 Without

DOWN

1 Aid for a maid
2 Metropolitan, e.g.
3 Scottish refusal
4 Sightseeing boat feature
5 Fancy headwear
6 Singer Brickell and others
7 Department store department
8 Utilities regulatory agcy.
9 Admired
10 D' ___-guerre (prewar): Fr.
11 Heads of Quebec
12 Relative of Manx
13 One way to be thrown
14 Ancient warship
19 Recent ex-con, maybe
23 They keep groups together
25 State clearly
26 "Bus Stop" star, 1955
29 Marquise de ___ (Louis XIV's second wife)
30 Past tenses
31 Late in flowering
33 Drew a graph
37 Made a little lower?
38 Aegean gulf
39 Silverdome team
40 Lange role in "Sweet Dreams"
42 Vet's employer: Abbr.
43 Busy
46 It's tired
48 Thurman of "Pulp Fiction"

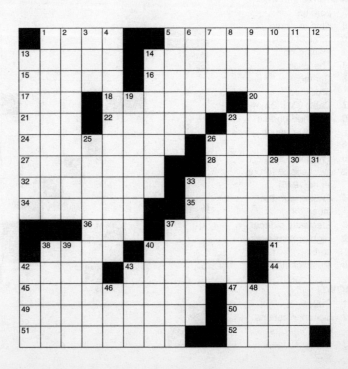

65

by Stephanie Spadaccini

ACROSS

1 Backs out
8 Descendant of Old Norse: Var.
15 Ham it up
16 Medicinal plants
17 1970 Picasso work, with "The"
18 Spectacles
19 Supermodel Carol
20 Walked through melted snow
22 Ratings org.
23 Invalid
25 Uninhabited
26 Cosmetics brand
27 Three-time Masters winner
29 Ballet's ___ de cheval
30 Teems
31 Votary
33 Giotto contemporary
34 Least likely to bend
36 Butler of literature
38 Numbskull
41 Reflective
42 Hackers' machines, for short
43 Pennies, sometimes
45 Dick Francis book "Dead ___"
46 Matches
48 Figure skater Thomas
49 Actress O'Connor
50 Sound of disapproval
52 Galoot
53 Similar to an apron top
55 Strengthen
57 Drooling
58 Most dreary

59 Moolah
60 Crosby's parish?

DOWN

1 "Friends" follower
2 1987 Isabel Allende novel
3 Stung
4 Baseball card stat.
5 Is a jet setter
6 ___ Militaire (Napoleon's alma mater)
7 Hussy
8 Encounters
9 J.P. Marquand's "The Late George ___"
10 "Alive" author Piers Paul
11 Where brass is made? Abbr.

12 Persuade to leave
13 Elizabeth's staff
14 Lamb specialties
21 Kirk Douglas role
24 Flickering
26 Struggle
28 Down's partner
30 Turkish official
32 Brand to dye for?
33 "___ Ring des Nibelungen"
35 TV Guide material
36 From Bonn or Cologne
37 Highly qualified for a job
39 Studio
40 "Clair de lune" composer
41 Goes diving
42 Portrait sitters
44 Glimpses

46 Actor Theodore
47 Show derision
50 Queen's domain
51 The fruit dove is its official bird
54 "Mighty ___ a Rose"
56 Scandinavian rug

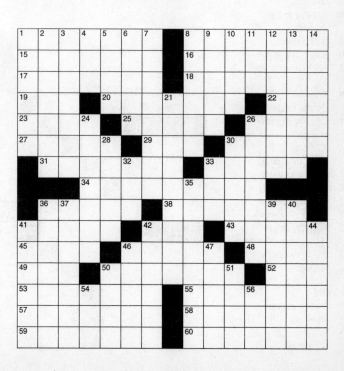

66

by Bob Klahn

ACROSS
1 Humbly
10 Well-versed
15 Kind of education
16 Dead letter, in post office talk
17 Barbara or Betty, once
18 It was East Pakistan's capital
19 Rate a ten
20 Hot, dry, Arabian wind
21 Work on something?
22 York, today
23 Just look
27 DNA triplet
28 Long rides?
29 Small, owner-operated
33 John of "Sands of Iwo Jima"
34 They're to be expected
35 Glib patter
36 Sourballs, e.g.
38 Fer-de-lance, for one
39 Recoils
40 Dental fixative
41 Literally, "golden orange"
44 "Cielo e ___!" (Ponchielli aria)
45 Here and there
46 Paid, informally
51 Galileo, for one
52 One's dealings?
53 Autumn colour
54 "The in-Laws" star
55 Big-time operator
56 Hopeless mess

DOWN
1 Platter player
2 Rah-rah
3 Whitewall, in Whitehall
4 She said "Play it, Sam!"
5 Money down?
6 Lighting compound
7 Staring
8 Botticelli's Venus, e.g.
9 "L.A. Law" co-star
10 Firedog
11 Financier Brady
12 De Niro in "Cape Fear"
13 Embroidery loop
14 Latin lover's words
20 Faceup cards in faro
22 One of Kipling's "Barrack-Room Ballads"
23 Dry-as-dust
24 Baryshnikov's birthplace
25 Persian cat?
26 Old-fashioned puzzle
27 Vintage cars
29 "Impression: Sunrise" artist
30 Kind of cleaner
31 Kind of cleaner
32 Chipper
34 Mythical river dweller
37 French connection?
38 Harvard's motto
40 Snarleyyow
41 "Batman" blow
42 TV's Spenser
43 One of Golda's colleagues
44 Back biter
46 First name in silents
47 Gross
48 Site along the Ijsselmeer
49 "The Haj" novelist
50 Shut in
52 Soul singer Cooke

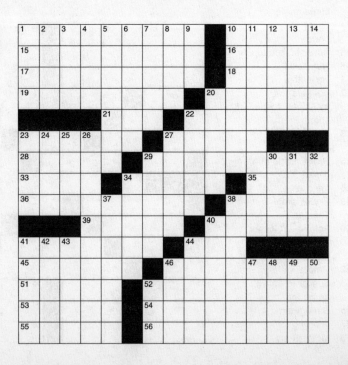

67

by Rand H. Burns

ACROSS

1 Taxidermist's item
7 Hawaiian for "long"
10 Covent Garden performer
14 Give
15 Three-footed
17 Edda author ___ Sturluson
18 Two-time British P.M.
19 "In the Heat of the Night" setting
21 Knotty
22 Ellery Queen, e.g.
25 Lace accommodator
26 Disposed
29 How to play a dirge
30 Language derived from Esperanto
31 Deighton's "Only When I ___"
33 Met
34 Arabic figure
37 Touching
39 Lack of clarity
41 Reason
42 Yukon, e.g.: Abbr.
44 Maintain
45 Feminine subject
46 Cyberspace service
48 Full-house sign
49 Comics character since 1929
51 Summery
53 Woody vine
55 Rio Grande city
58 "May I present . . ."
61 Vacuum-tube type
63 Absence of a body part
64 Early geometer
65 Rolls
66 Celebrated boy-king
67 Pirate's wear

DOWN

1 Literary inits.
2 Cariou and Dawson
3 Drenched
4 Use corporal punishment in a way
5 Light chestnut
6 Court testifier
7 Bygone Ford
8 ". . . ___ shall die"
9 River to the Oíse
10 Marksman
11 Communism and others
12 Utility
13 Favored set
16 Money maker
20 Actress Bening et al.
23 Bolted down
24 Disneyland feature
26 "___, poor Milan!": Prospero
27 Leaf
28 Eventuated
30 Cretan summit
32 Camera accessory
35 Appian Way, e.g.
36 Mistranscription
38 Born
40 Gardner's Paul Drake, e.g.
43 Ambulance crew member: Abbr.
47 Thrash
49 "Nonsense!"
50 Resistance figure
51 Take up space
52 German camera
54 Wow
56 Cabbagehead
57 Of Pindar's work
59 English sky-god
60 Presidential inits.
62 Crossed "d" letter

by Nancy Joline

ACROSS

1 Impasses
11 Southern senator
15 Yielder
16 Fashion shade
17 Baloney
18 Bottom of the barrel
19 Connection
20 Muff
21 Boxer Griffith et al.
23 Mr. ___ of "The Wind in the Willows"
25 Detailed computer instructions
27 Plaudits
29 Game for the record books
30 One of a poetic eightsome
32 Ransom ___ Olds
33 Soc. Sec. recipients
34 Look
36 Vitamin C drinks
39 Pizzetti opera "___ Gherardo"
42 Ad ___
44 Bars
48 Empathize with
51 ___ Land (northern Greenland)
52 Not really that good
54 Critic's bestowal
55 Union
56 C.E.O., e.g.
58 Year in the Middle Ages
59 Countertenor
60 "Star Wars" or "Alien"
64 The Bee ___
65 Like some vehicles
66 Swirl
67 Trojans' home base

DOWN

1 Took off
2 Cook's thickener
3 Routes to the Supreme Court
4 Count Basie's "___ Darlin'"
5 Vacances time
6 Ruminate
7 Morning sound
8 Bullish
9 Letter abbr.
10 Type of leather
11 Survivor
12 Wild cats
13 Strain improver
14 Some restaurant workers
22 Miss Piggy's query
24 Morse code dashes
26 Fizzy drink
28 Kickoff point
31 Practice
35 Early feminist Lucretia
37 Subj. of psychological study
38 Geneviève and others: Abbr.
39 Roquefort, e.g.
40 Celebrated
41 Put on guard
43 Contemporaries
45 Haggis ingredient
46 Steppe
47 Aleppo residents
49 Fleet
50 Sei halved
53 Pronouncements
57 Hammer part
61 Hamas rival
62 Assn.
63 Grand ___ ("Evangeline" locale)

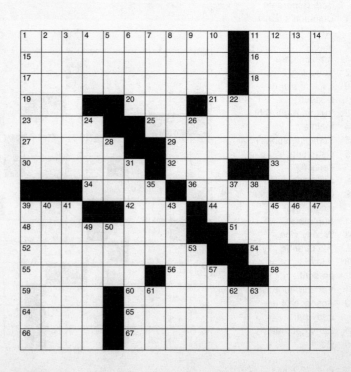

69

by Manny Nosowsky

ACROSS

1 1988 Dreyfuss-Julia comedy
16 Change direction
17 Joseph Conrad jungle tale
18 Field: Prefix
19 "The Lost World" author
20 Insignificant one
21 Shaquille O'Neal's alma mater: Abbr.
22 One in charge
24 Have an epiphany
25 Political grouping
26 "___ a Kick Out of You"
28 Examine, in Essex
31 Connects solidly
35 ___ cake
36 Live and breathe
37 Live for evil?
40 Mortars' mates
42 Corresponding
43 Hi's partner
44 Rank below capt.
47 Scout troop groups
49 Eng. station
52 Prissy
54 "Of ___ Sing"
55 Trundle
56 Treacly 1984 Disney movie
59 1970 Creedence Clearwater Revival hit
60 It helps a shopper say no

DOWN

1 Taj ___
2 Cassini and others
3 Hokkaido port
4 Poppaea's third husband
5 Crumb
6 Magic systems
7 Use the police
8 Color over
9 Like David's writing
10 Plot size
11 Korean soldier
12 Genealogy figure
13 Columnist Pearson et al.
14 Actor Davis
15 Remainder, in Rouen
22 Botanical snapper
23 Vengeance deified
25 Real property: Abbr.
27 Preacher's readings
28 Ethics-policing grp.
29 Saint Theresa was one
30 Santa ___

32 It's nothing at all
33 China's Lao ___
34 City map abbrs.
38 Do it yourselfer
39 Marsh gas, essentially
40 Much-bombed Romanian city of W.W. II.
41 Ancient flints
44 Middling grade
45 ___ hint (clue in)
46 Oppose
48 Foxx and namesakes
49 "The House in Paris" author Elizabeth
50 Noir's opposite
51 Jeremy of Chad and Jeremy
53 Just

55 Singer McEntire
57 Spanish article
58 Riled (up)

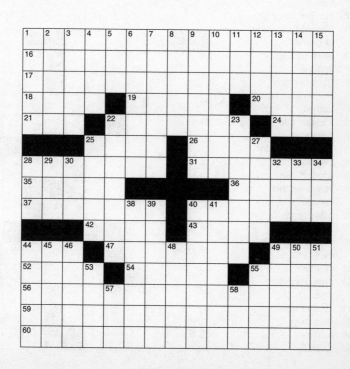

by Walter Webb

ACROSS

1 Aegean island, home of the despot Polycrates
6 "Quo Vadis?" garb
11 First sergeant, in military slang
13 Lenses
15 Type of supplement
16 Was jubilant
17 Org. for the Raiders, not the Rams
18 Guanacos
20 Bananas
21 Short-billed songbirds
23 TV producer Spelling
24 Tushingham of "Doctor Zhivago"
25 Pick
27 Tin Pan Alley grp.
28 Former teammate of Darryl
29 More chilling
31 Judges
34 Start of many Portuguese place names
35 Mideast title
36 Turncoat
41 Ardent supporter
45 Reverse
46 Clod
48 Home on the range
49 1944 Andy Russell hit
50 Film director Forman
52 "Franks"
53 Remote button: Abbr.
54 Cosa follower
55 Get away
56 Lucifer
58 Loblolly
61 Gerrymanders
62 Body toxin
63 Inveigle, in a way
64 Mouthwatering

DOWN

1 Phantasm
2 Alias lead-in
3 Summer's beginning
4 Florida city
5 Launch of 5/25/73
6 50's TV western, with "The"
7 Albatross
8 Evans of jazz
9 Crosby's "Blue Skies" partner
10 Court staff
11 Exactly
12 Recorded
13 Journal, for one
14 Paragons
19 First word of the "Aeneid"
22 Kind of tail
24 Took turns
26 Darker than turquoise
30 Robert, for one
32 Ger. state
33 "___ You Babe"
36 Vibration
37 Without emotional reaction
38 Hero-worship
39 Ear pollutants
40 "Atlas Shrugged" leader
42 "Mea culpa," at times
43 Delight
44 Managerial wimps
47 Arrangement
50 Change, in a way
51 Post-exercise relaxer
54 It's frowned upon
57 ___ cit.
59 Wino's affliction
60 Homer, e.g.

by Fred Piscop

ACROSS

1 Calculation aids
6 Dam
10 Outlaws
14 Athenian statesman
15 It's usually vaulted
16 Roll call eschewer
17 Slangy contraction
18 Like an oboe, but not a sax?
19 "Streamers" playwright
20 Eggheads
22 Prima ballerina
24 Site of Camus's "The Plague"
25 Ragtime dance
26 Rome capturer
29 Where to see Hawaii, perhaps
30 Item between a twin and a queen?
31 Water carriers
33 Makes dull
37 Utah Lake city
39 Chronic worry
41 Henhouse rarities
42 Its capital is Innsbruck
44 Trouble
46 Alpine stream
47 Crazies
49 Packed in
51 ___ Islands (Indian Ocean locale)
54 Tackle
55 Like some veterinary practice
56 Dedicated
60 "Kiss the Boys Goodbye" writer
61 Couples' hotel accommodation?
63 Blackboard holder
64 Roaster's place
65 "Johnny's Theme" co-writer
66 Pahlavi, e.g.
67 Bottom
68 Refusals
69 "The Highwayman" penner

DOWN

1 Fictional pooch
2 Defunct airline
3 Inter___
4 Baldheaded bird
5 Provisional
6 ___ Commission
7 Their points are covered
8 "Got it"
9 Becomes embarrassed
10 Pressure regulator
11 Look for
12 Like some gases
13 "O magic ___!": Keats
21 Portuguese territory
23 Be fertile
25 Assault
26 Prior's superior
27 Smelling a rat, perhaps
28 Viper
29 Quechua speakers
32 Actress Graff
34 Gang up on, as in basketball?
35 French 101 verb
36 Storage site
38 Most outmoded
40 Greyhound, e.g.
43 Butcher's cut
45 Old car, maybe
48 Stampeded
50 Citation jockey
51 Fuses
52 Pharmacists' solutions
53 Saint ___ (U.N. member since 1979)
54 Third items in series
56 School alternative
57 Anthem's start
58 Lacoste of tennis
59 Skull and Bones members
62 Mrs. Chaplin

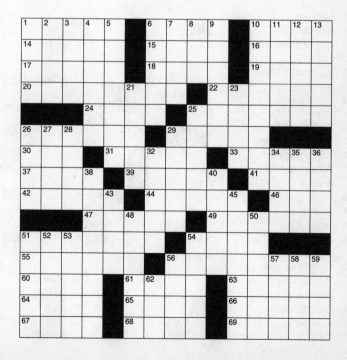

by A. J. Santora

ACROSS

1 Headword
6 Port of Spain
11 Vacation
13 Cremona craftings
15 First
16 Takes back, with "on"
18 Composer Bartók
19 Wrecking ball chore
21 Fasten, in a way
22 Romantic interlude
24 Kid's marble
25 Mayan food staple
27 Ferber size?
29 "Falstaff" composer
30 Kind of dye
33 Light's co-star in an 80's sitcom
35 Narrow-sleeved robes
36 Function
37 Nile delta city
40 Half of a half-and-half
41 "___ Ideas" (1950 hit)
43 Pointed arch
44 Raw
45 Pound and Stone
47 Grimm character
49 "___ beam up" ("Star Trek" phrase)
50 Hosp. printout
51 Sophisticated
55 Greek letter
56 Combined
59 Acting award
60 Certain secrets
62 Fidgety
64 Halo
65 Quit the union
66 Approvals
67 Fare

DOWN

1 Like graph paper
2 Johnny Mercer song
3 Mercury and others
4 Me, to Mimi
5 Way out there
6 West Indies native
7 Corner response
8 1964 Roger Miller hit
9 Zinc finish
10 Best-selling author on salesmanship
11 To you: Lat.
12 Bahamian nester
14 Like property under a court order
17 Scattered, old style
20 Went like lightning?
23 Poland's second-largest city
26 Pie ___ mode
28 Sheep talk
30 Soloist's number
31 Dangerous chess situation
32 In an oppressive way
34 1993 P.G.A. champ Paul and family
38 Nobelist Andric
39 Pearls
42 Edge a doily
46 "Three's Company" star
48 Waxed perfervid
50 Maxwell et al.
52 Conform to, with "by"
53 Fork and mouth locale
54 ___ off (angry)
57 Northeast Indian
58 Open-season quest
61 Calamity
63 School subj.

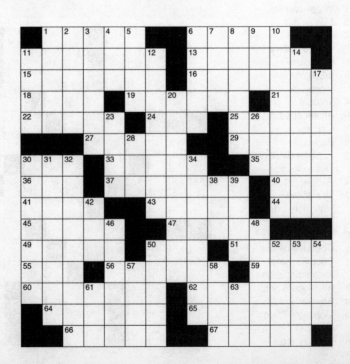

73

by Bob Klahn

ACROSS

1. Rudimentary stages
8. Loser to Herbert Hoover
15. "Measure for Measure" character
16. "War and Peace" heroine
17. Flipped out
18. Plant too much
19. It's spotted in the woods
20. Readily predictable
21. Cartoonist Chast
22. Relative of the lemming
24. Butcher shop buys
25. Blueprint detail
27. Utopia, literally
30. Rowdydows
32. Filibuster
33. 1970's discipline
36. "Butterfield 8" Oscar winner
39. Triple Crown jockey Turcotte
40. In __ (from a lab)
41. Crosby's record label
42. Get back on
44. Nice bread
45. Spooks
48. Biz biggies
50. Family members
51. Family members
54. Tarnish
56. Away, in a way
57. Body __
58. Attitudes
59. Queen's University site
60. Tomboys
61. Nods

DOWN

1. "Howards End" novelist
2. Favorite of Kublai Khan
3. Arrived airily
4. Muscat moolah
5. Comic Smirnoff
6. About 907 kilograms
7. Crushed
8. Mr. X, for short
9. Deterge
10. Reinforced, in a way
11. Gortner of "Falcon Crest"
12. Ichikawa immigrant
13. Annoyance
14. Advertises
20. Stayed on top (of)
23. Be beaten by
26. Bro
28. Punjab capital
29. High, in music
31. Avoids embarrassment
33. Yosemite peak
34. Bolshevik
35. Cuts across
37. Catcher behind the plate?
38. Ozarks O.K.
42. Forward
43. Old fogies
45. Smidgen
46. Scout, for one
47. Champlevé
49. Unloads
52. Tandoor
53. Subtracting
55. "Spirit of '76" instrument
57. Striking grp.

by Alex K. Justin

ACROSS

1 Kind of guide
7 Everyday
13 More unsavory
14 Superimpose
16 Tchaikovsky opera
17 Noted Miami villa and garden
18 Has an idea
19 "___ Lisa"
20 Ebenezer's snub
21 Popular dolls
22 Beside oneself
24 "Metaphysics of Morals" author
25 Centimeter-gram-second unit
26 Haute ___ (style of horse training)
27 Morticia's husband
28 Go against
29 Search far and wide
30 It may be indefinite
33 Unhinge
34 Noted test-marketing site
35 Parthenope, for one
36 Gave the glad eye
37 Bow's opposite
38 Voracious appetite
41 Schubert specialty
42 Deep felt
43 Bye
44 Garry Moore vocalist Denise
45 Steve McQueen's first major movie, with "The"
46 Hitches, so to speak
48 Painting the town red
50 Royal servants of old
51 Fill up

52 Directly toward sunup
53 Money broker
54 Motionless

DOWN

1 Former
2 Risky campus activity
3 Idyllic locales
4 In one's prime
5 Drink since 1898
6 Notre Dame name of fame
7 Nay
8 Sheeplike
9 Iran's Mohammed ___ Pahlevi
10 Perry Como, affectionately
11 Mobile home dweller?

12 Bomb
13 Cure, in a way
15 Popular dice game
19 Foamy drink
23 Bounder
24 It contains 114 suras
26 Rodrigo Díaz de Bivar
27 Bridge authority
28 Put in a kiln
29 Uncover diligently
30 1960's–70's flights
31 Important basketball tournament
32 Bear
33 Balanced regimen
35 Proof of attendance
37 Musicographer

38 Family V.I.P.'s
39 Optimally
40 "That ___ so bad"
42 Having wings
43 Pupil
45 Bit of sweat
47 Garden hand
49 10th-anniversary gift
50 Many seek its approval: Abbr.

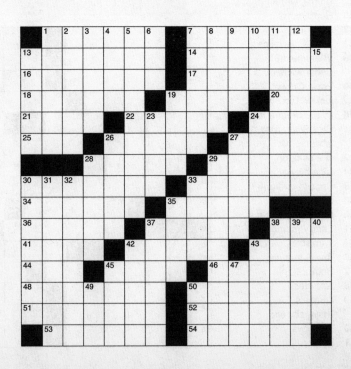

by Fred Piscop

ACROSS

1 60's TV home
10 Put together
15 Not derived from plants or animals: Var.
16 Jazzman Chick
17 Grounds
18 Cronus or Oceanus, e.g.
19 Put in position
20 It's a blast
21 Philosophy of patient care
22 Uneven
24 ___ Tass (Russian news agency)
26 Half a dance?
27 Dictator's security force, perhaps
30 Hammer wielder
31 High-tech defense inits.
34 Puppeteer Lewis et al.
35 Actress Loughlin of "Full House"
36 1968 one hit wonder
38 Grease up
40 Cinema canine
41 Prepare for market
43 "___ Beso" (1962 hit)
44 Remain in the shadows
45 Seaport in 59-Across
47 90's singer ___ Kamoze
48 Former New Jersey Governor Thomas
49 As ___ Methuselah
53 Wounded by the barber
55 Prohibitionist's foe
58 "Scarface" star, 1932
59 Leghorn locale
60 ___ hour (prayer time)
62 Stiff hairs
63 Rival of Smell-O-Vision, in Hollywood
64 Election night development
65 Conventioneers

DOWN

1 It comes with a title
2 Studio sign
3 "What's ___ like?"
4 Oenophile's superlative
5 Much-bruised item
6 Bombast
7 ___ impulse
8 More filled with fine sand
9 Golf coup
10 Part man?
11 Drudge
12 It may have a good heart
13 Coasts
14 Europe's oldest independent country
21 Annoys
23 Dummy position
25 Sibelius's "Valse ___"
28 Geared up, perhaps
29 Ballerina Karsavina
30 R.N.'s dispense it
31 Hard-liner of old
32 Alienator
33 Knotty
37 Chew the fat
39 Division word
42 Not the fanciest eating utensils
46 Upstate New York city
48 Excited, with "up"
50 Admission requirement
51 "What's in ___?"
52 George Eliot character
54 Hateful group
56 Hydroxyl compound
57 Bartlett's Familiar Quotations, e.g.
60 Hardly Mr. Right
61 Plague

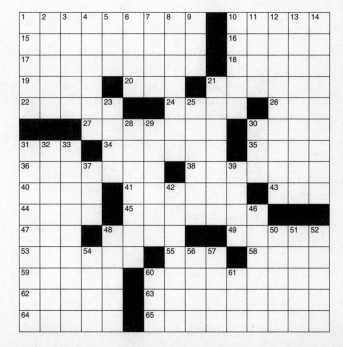

NOW AVAILABLE!

THE FIRST BOOK OF ITS KIND!

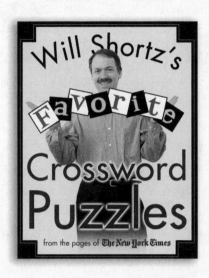

"Will Shortz, crossword editor of *The New York Times*,
is [the crossword book world's] John Grisham."—Martin Arnold

"The Riddler's got nothing on Will Shortz"—*Time Out* (New York)

▪ Seventy-five of Will Shortz's favorite crossword puzzles from the pages of *The New York Times* ▪

▪ Special commentary on why each puzzle belongs among his favorites ▪

▪ Two-page introduction ▪

So sharpen your pencil and be prepared for the most interesting,
witty, and fun puzzles from the pages of *The New York Times!*

1

```
D E S K T O P ■ T R A D E I N
E X T E R N E ■ R I S O T T O
B A R N Y A R D E P I T H E T
A M A T ■ N U R S E ■ H I R E
S P Y ■ ■ S A T ■ ■ C A P
E L E C ■ F A B L E ■ T A T A
R E D R I L L ■ E N S I L E D
■ ■ A B E ■ ■ J O T ■ ■
S A B I N E S ■ P O L A R I S
A L A N ■ T A R R Y ■ N A C L
W D S ■ ■ T A I ■ ■ D E A
D E E P ■ L I K E A ■ L I D S
U N D E R O N E S B R E A T H
S T O R A G E ■ T R A I N E E
T E N F O O T ■ S I E S T A S
```

2

```
T A C O M A ■ G I G O L O S
E L I D E D ■ O N L E A V E
A U T O E D ■ S H O R T E N S
S M A R T ■ P L E A ■ C R A W
E N D S ■ S H I R T ■ H A T E
D I E ■ A T O N E ■ T O P
■ L O V I N G ■ A V E R T
■ H E R O ■ J I V E ■
S W I M S ■ F U R I E S
P A M ■ T O N E D ■ N O S
E N I D ■ C R O C S ■ S A R I
A N T I ■ H A L O ■ R E R A N
R E A C T I V E ■ L I V I N G
■ S T E A M E R ■ A V E N G E
■ T E R S E L Y ■ M E R G E R
```

3

```
D R A G ■ P E T I T ■ S L U R
A U R A ■ A G E N A ■ K Y R A
F R O M C T O S H I N I N G C
T A M E R S ■ L A L A ■ N E E
■ L A D E ■ A L O N E ■
■ P A L ■ E R U D I T E
A C H I E V E R ■ E T R E
B L E S S E D R T H E M E E K
B O L L ■ S U R N A M E S
A T L A S E S ■ N S W
■ M O R E S ■ R O M E
S O B ■ L A T H ■ S A R A N S
T H E B O S T O N T P A R T Y
A I D E ■ E L E N A ■ L I E N
N O S E ■ S E D E R ■ S O R E
```

4

```
P E T E R A R N O ■ J A M A
I S O L A T I O N ■ S A L E S
S T R I K E O U T ■ T W I N S
H O T S E A T S ■ P E B B L E
■ S S S ■ B A R R I O S
M A S H I E ■ B O R N E
I N C A N ■ Q U I T E A B I T
C Z A R ■ D U L L Y ■ K E N O
H A N D R A I L S ■ P E T A L
■ K E N T S ■ E R R A N D
P L A N E T S ■ M A I
R E M O V E ■ P A R T H R E E
O N I C E ■ H I T T H E H A Y
M I N K S ■ O N T H E N O S E
O N E S ■ P O S S E S S E D
```

5

```
I S A A C ■ E A P ■ S A R D I
M A R T H A S V I N E Y A R D
A L I M E N T A R Y C A N A L
N E Z ■ A W E S O M E ■ D Y E
■ S T A R ■ U P D O ■
■ L A M E R ■ R E H E A R S
A U G U R ■ R E T O R T I O N
F L O G ■ R U N T S ■ B L U E
B U R G L A R E E ■ C R E P T
■ S A L I V A S ■ S H A D Y
■ E M I L ■ G M A N ■
F L U ■ N O I S I E R ■ S R I
R U M P E L S T I L T S K I N
E X P E R I M E N T A T I O N
T E S T S ■ S T G ■ E A S T S
```

6

```
. S T A L K . . P A S S O S
S T A T I N G . A C T O N E
C A S H M E R E . R E P U T E
O P T . N E E D L E S . V H S
O L E G . L E W I S . F E E T
P E R E S . N A B . D I N G O
. . T H E P R E S I D I O
. S L A V E D R I V E R
. S H O R E P A T R O L
C H O S E . P L Y . T I A R A
H A R T . R E B B E . O R A L
A P T . C A R E E N S . M N O
S E A D O G . E L D O R A D O
E U G E N E . L E B A N O N
S P E W E D . D E N I M .
```

7

```
E M E N D . A T A T . L E A R
B A Y O U . C A M A R I L L A
B R E V E . H U P M O B I L E
. . E S P Y . L A I R .
S M I L E R . F E R . E S A U
E O N . N I T A . A T T A I N
W A S H B O A R D . E T Y M A
. P I E R C E A R R O W .
S H I R R . O W N E R S H I P
I R R E G S . A S E A . E R A
N E E D . E A R . S P I N E T
. G I L D . E E L S .
S P A U L D I N G . A L V I N
S T I N K E R O O . N A I V E
W A R S . S E T S . E M M E T
```

8

```
S H R O V E . S L O B B E R S
C O I N E R . N O N F A T A L
A M P E R E . A P O L L O I I
R E P A Y . S P A . A L I N E
F I L L . C A P T . T O L E R
A N I . Z A N Y . . T E D
C O N J U R E . A R A B .
E N G I N E S . C O R O N A S
. M I S T . Q U I X O T E
. H U H . R U E D . T Y E
J O N E S . G A I N . Z A P S
A R E N T . O P T . P E T I T
P A S S E S U P . A L P A C A
A C C O L A D E . P O P L A R
N E O N A T A L . A T O L L S
```

9

```
D A D A . S C A M . A B A C K
E T O N . O L G A . C A L L A
V E N T I D I U S . O N T A P
O N A I R . P E T R U C H I O
. . P E E P . E O S . O R K
B A S H . M E R R I T T .
O L I O . U R I . L I O N E L
B E L L I . S P A . C U O M O
S C O U R S . E R R . C L I O
. S O L A R I A . H O L T
A T A . N O D . D E B S .
D O N A L B A I N . A T A R I
A D I E U . G L E N D O W E R
R A M O N . E S S O . N E N A
E Y I N G . S A S S . E D E N
```

10

```
J A M E S C A A N . F L A M
A T A G L A N C E . P R A T E
D I N G A L I N G . L A U R A
A T N O T I M E . H A N D I N
. . . I C E . W I N K S A T
C A S I N O . L I L A C .
O W I N G . T O P D R A W E R
P A T H . T Y P E A . P O L O
E Y E O P E N E R . P R O A M
. . T O P A Z . C R A D L E
S N O W S I N . T A E .
H E S A I D . P E N C H A N T
O R A T E . R O S C O E L E E
E D G E S . I S L E O F M A N
D Y E R . C H A L K T A L K
```

11

```
  A R C H L Y     S I L K S
A L O H A O E   S T R I A T E
S I L O I N G   L E I P Z I G
K I E R K E G A A R D   A R G
      D U N   S T N I C K
S A K S   E P T   E U C H R E
W I N     S E A S   M U S E R
A D A   H S T   I D S   T I N
M A C R O   E D G E     A G E
I N K I N D   I N S   A N N S
    W A G E R S   O L D
A B U   K N U C K L E H E A D
P U R L O I N   R A V E L L Y
E S S E N E S   I T E R A T E
  S T A G S     S E L E N E
```

12

```
P O U L E N C   G R I M A C E
A N N U L A R   O E D I P A L
P R O V I S O   O B O V A T E
H A W   E A S E F U L   R A M
O M N I   L S M F T   D E L I
S P E N T   T U T   T O J O S
  S D E A T H   H E R Z O G
    R U S E   E R I E
  P A T T E R   D A M N E D
J E L L O   U S E   S T R I P
A R M Y   A B I E S   H U L A
L O A   F L I P P E D   D U G
A R A M A I C   E D O M I T E
P A T E R N O   N E G A T E R
A L A T E E N   D R Y N E S S
```

13

```
  T O P O L   E S C A P A D E
T H R I V E   S T A I R W A Y
A E G E A N   P A R D O N M E
B E A T L E S   T R E S S E S
S T N     O B E Y S
  E L S   E F O R     H I J
B R O K E R A G E H O U S E S
I N F A N T R Y G E N E R A L
N A T I V E A M E R I C A N S
  L S T     S A N D   O E S
      P A I N T     L D S
T I E B A C K   S U S P I R E
I N D O L E N T   S T A T E N
S K E L E T O N   M E R E S T
H A N D D O W N   A M A S S
```

14

```
S P A N I E L   P R I S O N S
T A B A S C O   H O N A L E E
E D I T I O N   Y I E L D E D
A R D E N   G B S   Z E L D A
L O I S   E L L I S   M I L T
T N N   G R O U C H O   N E E
H I G H R I S E   A C C E S S
      M I N T J U L E P
U N H O L Y   E N L A R G E D
T E E   L E B A N O N   E V E
O V I D   S I N E W   S O I L
P E R E Z   T S E   M A L L E
I R E P E A T   D A S B O O T
A B S O L V E   E P E R G N E
H E S T L E R   D E C A Y E D
```

15

```
P I P E T T E   S P L I T U P
R A I N H A T   O R I S O N S
E N T R A N T   N O M O N E Y
    B A N G U P J O B   T A C
R O U G E     O A F   W I T H
A B L E   M A P   S W A N E E
N I L   L O B B Y   A N E N D
    B A M B O O Z L E
S P L A T   E T H E L   S P A
T E A R E D   T O N   S W A M
J A M B   I S L   F E E L S
A S I   P O W E R T R I P
M A N M A D E   O R E S T E S
E N A C T E D   B E R M U D A
S T R A S S E   S E E S P O T
```

16

	H	E	R	B		O	V	E	R	I	C	E
	S	E	W	E	R		R	A	M	A	D	A	S
	B	A	R	E	B	A	C	K	R	I	D	E	R	S
G	A	L	O	R	E		U	N	I	T		N	I	E
E	T	T	E		L	U	T	E		S	A	T	O	N
N	O	O	S	E		L	A	Y	S		L	I	C	E
A	R	F		C	L	A	N		A	R	E	C	A	S
	T	I	C	O	N	D	E	R	O	G	A	
S	C	H	L	E	P		D	O	I	T		L	E	W
T	A	E	L		E	C	R	U		E	N	T	R	Y
O	B	E	Y	S		H	I	S	S		A	W	E	S
M	O	A		O	B	I	E		T	O	P	I	C	S
P	O	R	T	L	A	N	D	C	E	M	E	N	T
E	S	T	R	A	D	A		H	E	I	R	S	
R	E	H	I	R	E	S		A	R	T	Y

17

S	H	A	C	K		H	O	L	D	S	O	V	E	R
T	I	T	A	N		A	B	O	U	T	T	I	M	E
E	N	T	R	E		L	O	O	S	E	E	N	D	S
A	G	A	P	E		L	I	N	T		A	G	E	E
M	E	R	E		M	O	S	S	E	D		T	N	T
		N	E	T	W	T		R	U	B	
H	O	S	T	A	G	E	S		M	A	Y	A	S
I	N	H	E	R	E	D		J	O	B	L	E	S	S
P	E	A	R	L		R	A	B	E	L	A	I	S
		S	A	T		E	M	E	R	Y	
D	R	J		P	A	S	S	B	Y		H	A	H	A
R	O	O	M		P	I	C	O		C	O	Z	E	N
A	S	I	A	M	I	N	O	R		H	O	U	N	D
G	I	N	G	E	R	A	L	E		E	E	R	I	E
S	E	T	S	A	S	I	D	E		T	R	E	E	S

18

	D	E	C	A	F			R	E	P	O	S	E
M	A	L	A	D	I	E	S		E	L	O	P	E	S
E	V	A	N	E	S	C	E		A	S	L	E	E	P
T	E	L	E	P	H	O	N	E	C	A	L	L	S	
		T	E	N	A	N	T	
	C	U	E		S	O	T	T	O	V	O	C	E
P	A	P	A	L		M	E	R	R	I	M	E	N	T
C	L	O	S	E	B	Y		E	S	P	A	R	T	O
B	E	N	E	D	I	C	T	A		S	N	E	E	R
	B	A	D	S	T	A	R	T	S		I	S	R
		T	R	U	M	A	N	
	M	O	V	I	E	S	C	E	N	A	R	I	O	S
L	A	M	A	R	R		E	N	D	T	O	E	N	D
A	T	R	I	A	L		S	T	R	E	S	S	E	S
W	H	I	N	N	Y		A	S	S	T	S	

19

	J	O	S	S		J	A	L	I	S	C	O
	S	O	U	T	H		A	U	D	I	T	O	R	S
S	T	E	R	E	O		S	M	A	R	T	I	E	S
T	A	I		P	O	R	K	P	I	E		L	A	I
U	R	S	A		S	A	F	E	R		M	E	T	E
B	L	U	M	E		P	O	D		S	I	D	E
S	I	Z	E	T	H	I	R	T	E	E	N	
	T	U	R	N	E	D	T	H	E	T	I	D	E
	C	A	N	T	H	E	C	O	M	E	D	Y
	T	R	E	S		R	E	G		N	U	B	I	A
F	O	O	D		R	A	M	U	S		M	A	T	H
O	U	T		C	A	N	O	N	I	C		T	O	O
I	S	T	H	A	T	S	O		T	O	R	E	R	O
S	L	E	E	P	S	I	N		E	V	E	R	S	
T	E	N	S	P	O	T		D	E	B	S	

20

S	P	A	R	E	P	A	R	T	S		V	A	R
T	O	M	A	T	O	S	O	U	P		E	L	E	M
R	E	A	L	E	S	T	A	T	E		R	A	J	A
A	T	T	E	S	T	E	D		W	I	S	D	O	M
P	I	E	S		S	R	I	S		N	A	D	I	A
I	C	U			E	L	A	S	T	I	C	S
N	A	R	R	O	W	S		A	L	P	I	N	E
		E	C	H	O		T	O	O	L	
	A	C	E	T	A	L		E	U	T	E	R	P	E
A	R	O	M	A	T	I	C			A	R	R
H	A	G	E	N		D	A	T	A		G	L	E	N
O	M	E	R	T	A		D	I	S	S	O	L	V	E
L	A	N	G		T	R	E	A	S	U	R	I	E	S
D	I	C	E		E	N	T	R	A	P	M	E	N	T
	C	Y	D		E	S	S	A	Y	T	E	S	T	S

21

```
  U N O   A F T   R E B
  S T U F F E D O L I V E S
L I T T L E G R E Y C E L L S
A L E   A D E   P R O   L Y E
W O R T   E A G L E   O I S E
    H E R N I A   A R C
C A S A V A   S T A N D O U T
U R A N I T E   E R N E S T O
R E C K L E S S   T U R E E N
    R E S   P O W E L L
S E E D   D E W A R   Y M C A
O D D   T E C   X I S   E A R
S A C R I F I C I A L L A M B
  M O U N T A I N L I O N S
    W R Y   L A G   P O T
```

22

```
  G R O W T H   J U J I T S U
A R A P A H O   E P O C H A L
C A T A R R H   W A C K I L Y
T N T   N O O N E   K E N T S
A G R I   W H E L P   S K I S
S E A R S   O W L E T   E N E
  S P A T E   M E A S U R E S
      N O N V E R B A L
S U B I N D E X   O R N O T
E P A   Y U R I S   S A B I N
E T R E   P I C A S   E L S A
H I R E D   T O M E S   I S M
E M E R I T I   B R U S Q U E
R E T I R E E   A V E N U E S
E S T E E M S   R E D O E S
```

23

```
S H O P   F O U R S Q U A R E
L E N T   O E D I P U S R E X
A R E A   I N I T I A T I V E
P B A   E L O N   T R A D E
S I T   R E N E W E R
T V A   A D E   A F E A R D
I O T A S   A D U L T E R Y
C R I T   M A B E L   O G E E
K E M O S A B E   T R I A L
  S E M P R E   I S A   M D L
    L I T E R A L   E L O
  T A P I N   L O L L   N O W
C O P A C A B A N A   E T C S
I T I N E R A T E D   W A K E
D E S T R O Y E R S   E L S A
```

24

```
B O D E   - O F P E P P E R
A V I D E   E N A R R I E R E
L E V E L   R E L E G A T E S
D R U M S   T S P S   A C T
E L L A   V E E S   R T S
R A G   A S I R   S I D
- I E L L H A M M E T T
  D R E B I N   I N A S E A
    H U N D R E D Y A R D -
  A I M   E N O S   R O B
S C D   S T U S   C A P O
T O V   S L A T   M A N T A
I C E P L A N T S   I N T E R
C O R R U P T E R   B A I R D
H A B E R - E R S   L A S S
```

25

```
  S C A R F S   T Y B A L T
  W A R H O L   R A L L Y E
C O R P O R A T E R A I D E R
A L P   S T Y R E N E   D N A
C L O P   W E A N S   M I I I
H E R O   A R I A   L A T E N
E N T I T Y   L I B E L E R S
    S A N D B L A S T
A R B O R E A L   T H E M A N
T E R N S   T A F T   S A R I
I L E S   B E Z E L   E R I K
L E A   D E L E T E D   L E E
T A K E O V E R T A R G E T S
  S I E V E S   E X E U N T
  E N G E L S   R E D S E A
```

26

```
S T O R M S O F F ■ ■ ■ N O V
W A K E U P C A L L ■ D A B O
E N C H I L A D A S ■ I T L L
A Z O ■ R I S ■ U P S H O T
T A R P ■ T E R M ■ A M A N A
E N R O L ■ Y E A R N I N G
R I A T A S ■ P R O D S ■
S A L A B L E ■ T W O S O M E
■ T O A L L ■ E R I V A N
■ C H O R T L E S ■ A N E N T
P R I C E ■ S A N E ■ G R O H
F U C H R E ■ A X L ■ C L U
T I K I ■ S L O P P Y J O E S
A S O P ■ P E R P E T U A T E
L E K ■ D A Y L E T T E R
```

27

```
■ R O B U S T ■ B L A M I N G
D E V I L L E ■ L A B O R E R
O P E N A I R ■ U P C L O S E
S U R ■ N E R V E ■ D A N S E
E T A S ■ R O O M S ■ R A I N
D E G A S ■ R I O T S ■ G E E
■ D E L T A ■ C O U N T E S S
■ T A I L E N D E R ■
T R I S T R A M ■ Y E A S T
R O N ■ S E N A T ■ S C A R E
O M N I ■ S T I E S ■ E L U L
M A I N S ■ E L S A S ■ T A I
P I N E T A R ■ T I E P I N S
I N G R O W N ■ E N T E N T E
N E S T L E S ■ E T A P E S ■
```

28

```
E L E V E N T H S ■ S P A D E
R O S E M A R I E ■ E L B O W
I N A N I M A T E ■ N A I V E
N E U T R A L S ■ R A I D E R
■ A T A ■ W I T N E S S
L E N G T H ■ W I D O W ■
I S D U E ■ T O L E R A N T
E S A I ■ C O R M S ■ T A O S
■ O K L A H O M A ■ F E S T A
■ L S A T S ■ C O R T E X
A P R O P O S ■ T A X ■
B A S T E S ■ S U N L O V E R
O P T I C ■ P A T T I P A G E
V A U N T ■ I N T O K E N O F
E L V E S ■ N O I S E L E S S
```

29

```
C A R T I L A G E ■ S T U B
A L I E N A T E D ■ T H E R E
W A T E R P O L O ■ B U R G S
S E A M O U N T ■ B O T R E E
■ A T E ■ C O N T E S T
A M A N D A ■ G R A D E ■
C U B E S ■ B R A S S R I N G
A I L S ■ A L O F T ■ B O O M
D R E S S I E S T ■ L U N G E
■ E A R N S ■ P I G E O N
S P E L L E D ■ T A N ■
T O R R I D ■ F I R E B A L L
A P R O N ■ L A G U A R D I A
S P O D E ■ E N E R G I Z E S
H A L E ■ A G R E E M E N T
```

30

```
W E S T W A L L ■ C I L I A
A M O R E T T O ■ T O N I N G
G A M E L E S S ■ W R A S S E
O N E A T A ■ P O P S T A R
N A T T E R ■ D U B ■ T E N S
E T H E R ■ N A Z A R E N E
R E I D ■ B U Z Z S A W S
S S N ■ M U Z Z L E D ■ T I A
■ G R I Z Z L E S ■ T O P I
■ F R A Z Z L E D ■ C O R E R
A R O N ■ A E R ■ R O B E R T
M A T T E R S ■ E N L A C E
U N T I E D ■ L A C T A S E S
S C E N E S ■ A L T A M O N T
T O N G S ■ D E S C E N T S
```

31

```
G A S P U M P ■ Q U I P P E D
A M N E S I A ■ U P S C A L E
W A I T E R S ■ E P I S T L E
A N D ■ R E S C U E S ■ B E D
I D E S ■ D E L E D ■ P O R E
N A R C O ■ D I D ■ P R O B E
■ A L S O P ■ A L O N E
■ G O L D E N J U B I L E E
■ I N D E X ■ O N E N O
S U P E R ■ M I G ■ K N I S H
C L A D ■ B O N U S ■ G O T O
R I T ■ P U N T I N G ■ D A N
E A R R I N G ■ D A Y T I M E
A N O I N T S ■ E R M I N E S
M I L D E S T ■ D E S C E N T
```

32

```
A C I ■ L I L A C ■ L A P I S
T A C ■ I N I G O ■ A B I D E
T R E ■ M O N E Y N I C K E L
A L C A N ■ O R D E A L
C O O L E D ■ C E O ■ M S S
H A L F D O L L A R A G E
E D D ■ F O E S ■ D I N
■ I N F L A T I O N
A C E ■ I V E S ■ D O A
Q U A R T E R N S I O N S
A B U ■ O A R ■ T A R G E T
P L A S M A ■ I R E N A
P U M P E R D I M E S ■ A E R
A M A I N ■ O R O N O ■ R S T
L E N T O ■ M A N O N ■ S S E
```

33

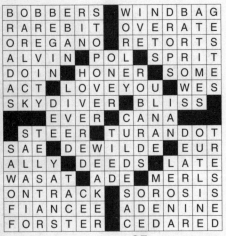

```
B O B B E R S ■ W I N D B A G
R A R E B I T ■ O V E R A T E
O R E G A N O ■ R E T O R T S
A L V I N ■ P O L ■ S P R I T
D O I N ■ H O N E R ■ S O M E
A C T ■ L O V E Y O U ■ W E S
S K Y D I V E R ■ B L I S S
■ E V E R ■ C A N A
■ S T E E R ■ T U R A N D O T
S A E ■ D E W I L D E ■ E U R
A L L Y ■ D E E D S ■ L A T E
W A S A T ■ A D E ■ M E R L S
O N T R A C K ■ S O R O S I S
F I A N C E E ■ A D E N I N E
F O R S T E R ■ C E D A R E D
```

34

```
S T R O M ■ V P S ■ S P A
C H A R O ■ D I E M ■ S P U R
R E D O N I O N R O M A I N E
A R I ■ T R U E ■ L I M N
P A C T ■ E G G S T O M A T O
E M C E E ■ H A L ■ S C O W
■ H E R A ■ R U B S ■ H O N
R A I S I N S C R O U T O N S
U F O ■ E T T U ■ Z E A L
M A C S ■ E C U ■ T R I C K
P R A W N S N U T S ■ O V A L
■ R A I L ■ M U N I ■ E R E
P A R S L E Y B R O C C O L I
U H O H ■ P E E N ■ O R I O N
G A T ■ T A R ■ N O L T E
```

35

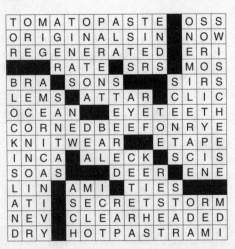

```
T O M A T O P A S T E ■ O S S
O R I G I N A L S I N ■ N O W
R E G E N E R A T E D ■ E R I
■ R A T E ■ S R S ■ M O S
B R A ■ S O N S ■ S I R S
L E M S ■ A T T A R ■ C L I C
O C E A N ■ E Y E T E E T H
C O R N E D B E E F O N R Y E
K N I T W E A R ■ E T A P E
I N C A ■ A L E C K ■ S C I S
S O A S ■ D E E R ■ E N E
L I N ■ A M I ■ T I E S
A T I ■ S E C R E T S T O R M
N E V ■ C L E A R H E A D E D
D R Y ■ H O T P A S T R A M I
```

36

```
V O I C E O V E R   A S S H E
I N T H E H O L E   S Q U I D
S T E E L M I L L   S U I N G
C O R D S   L A Y S   E S T A
E G A D   R E S   Q U A S A R
R E T A K E S   J U N K E T S
A N E R V E   H A I R Y
L Y S   E N Q U I R E   P A R
      S T A U B   R E S A V E
M O R O C C O   D E L E T E S
A R I G H T   G E L   A R N O
D I A G   S H E P   A L I G N
R E L I C   A N A A L I C I A
E N T E R   S O R E P O I N T
S T O R Y   P A T R O N A G E
```

37

```
R A P I N E   M E M O R I A L
E N A M O R   E X A M I N E E
P A L I N G   X E N O P H O N
A T O N E   V I R G O   A L A
N O M E   H E C T O   F L I P
E M I   A U R A S   G E E S E
L I N E S M A N   C A R
S C O T T I S H T E R R I E R
      H I D   A I R B O R N E
W O M E N   R I L E S   R T S
A R A L   E A R L S   D I R E
S I D   A R I L S   S A T A N
H O M E M A D E   S A V A N T
E L E V A T E S   E V I N C E
S E N A T O R S   T E S T E D
```

38

```
T H E B E A T L E S   S I G N
H O V E R C R A F T   A D E E
O P E N S H I R T S   L E S S
M E N   T E S S   O V E T T
A S I N         H A T E F U L
S O F A S   C R A B S   I R E
    N O T H E R E   E X E S
  D E A T H A N D T A X E S
D I A S   I N T A S T E
I S R   I N C A S   T R A M S
A R L E D G E       T R E E
G A Y L E   B A M A   I N N
R E M S   B I O L O G I S T S
A L A I   R O S E T A T T O O
M I N E   R I N G O S T A R R
```

39

```
  C A R E   P A L E F A C E
  C H I E N   I S A D O R A S
C H A R M S   Z W I E B A C K
Z O R B A   A Z A N   C H I
E L I A K A Z A N   S H E M
C L O S E S T   G O I N T O
H A T E   T E D   A B B E S S
        J A C U Z Z I
P O P L A R   O L E   M E T A
U P R I S E   O B E R L I N
R E E L   M O T O R B O A T
I N E   B U O Y   N O I R E
S T M O R I T Z   K A N S A S
T O I L E T T E   K N E E S
S E E D L E S S   K I S S
```

40

```
A L O P   M A P   W O R K
V E R A   S L I C E   A M I E
A M E R I C A N T R A G E D Y
    K N O U T S   G E N E S
N I S   U R N S   P A R
E N T E R E D   S I R   G O B
S C E N E   E R I E   D I C E
T H E O D O R E D R E I S E R
O O P S   D E L E   N O M A N
R N S   F E D   L A D R O N E
    B A R   L I R A   S S T
S C O R N   B O G G L E
A H O O S I E R H O L I D A Y
N O N O   D A R T S   R I L E
S W A M   A M Y   E D I T
```

41

A	N	A	L	O	G	I	S	T			T	A	R	P
R	A	R	E	E	A	R	T	H		B	A	L	E	R
D	I	M	E	S	T	O	R	E		A	K	I	T	E
O	V	E	R	T	O	N	E	S		L	E	T	A	T
R	E	D	Y	E		S	E	E		L	A	T	K	E
S	S	T				T	V	T	A	B	L	E	S	
	T	O	D	O	S		S	E	E	D	I	E	S	T
		I	V	E	D	O	N	E	I	T				
S	A	N	S	E	R	I	F		S	C	E	N	E	
P	R	E	T	R	I	A	L				O	A	T	
A	C	E	R	B		T	A	C		C	A	R	T	A
R	A	D	I	I		O	R	A	T	O	R	I	E	S
E	D	I	C	T		M	E	R	R	I	M	E	N	T
S	I	E	T	E		I	D	E	O	L	O	G	U	E
T	A	R	S			C	O	L	D	S	N	A	P	S

42

P	A	P	Y	R	I		J	I	M	I		E	R	A
A	T	R	A	I	N		A	N	A	L	Y	S	E	S
T	H	U	M	B	N	A	I	L	S	K	E	T	C	H
R	E	D	S		E	M	M	A	S		S	H	O	O
I	N	E		T	R	A	I	N	E	R		E	A	R
C	E	N	S	E		Z	E	D		E	A	R	L	E
E	U	C	L	A	S	E		S	K	I	T			
S	M	E	A	R	S			U	N	T	R	U	E	
		K	I	T	H		P	H	A	L	A	N	X	
L	A	D	E	N		E	L	A	N		E	M	I	T
A	R	A		G	E	T	I	T		H	E	A	V	E
U	R	N	S		N	A	S	H	U	A		D	E	N
P	I	C	T	U	R	E	P	O	S	T	C	A	R	D
E	V	E	R	M	O	R	E		F	L	E	N	S	E
R	E	S		A	L	A	R		L	O	O	S	E	D

43

	S	O	M	B	E	R		S	P	A	S	M	
S	Q	U	E	A	L	E	R		T	A	U	P	E	S
P	U	T	A	T	I	V	E		O	N	D	I	N	E
E	A	R	T	H	S		V	I	R	G	I	N	I	A
A	M	A	S	S		F	U	N	K		T	E	A	L
R	A	G			E	L	E	V		A	I	S	L	E
E	T	E		N	R	A		I	P	S	O			
D	A	S	H	I	N	G		C	A	T	N	A	P	S
		A	P	E	R		T	R	A		B	E	T	
E	D	E	N	S		A	Q	U	A		D	R	E	
L	E	N	D		O	N	U	S		O	L	I	V	E
M	A	R	I	E	T	T	A		A	M	I	C	A	L
E	L	I	C	I	T		R	E	N	E	G	A	D	E
R	E	C	A	N	E		K	N	I	G	H	T	E	D
	R	O	P	E	R		E	L	A	T	E	D		

44

C	A	T	S	P	A	J	A	M	A	S		M	A	A
A	N	A	C	H	R	O	N	I	S	M		I	T	S
L	A	K	E	O	N	T	A	R	I	O		C	T	S
	T	E	N	T	H			O	A	K	T	R	E	E
		T	O	E	D			T	E	N	O	N	S	
J	A	B	S		M	A	T	R	I		O	N	U	S
O	L	E				C	H	I	C		T	E	A	M
E	V	A	S		G	R	I	N	S		E	S	T	E
S	I	R	E		R	O	N	S				I	O	N
I	N	I	T		O	N	K	E	Y		C	A	R	T
X	A	N	A	D	U			S	E	H	R			
P	I	M	L	I	C	O		S	E	U	S	S		
A	L	I		T	H	R	E	E	M	A	S	T	E	R
C	E	N		T	E	A	R	S	A	R	O	U	N	D
K	Y	D		O	D	D	S	A	N	D	E	N	D	S

45

U	N	C	U	T			C	E	L	L	S	
P	E	L	A	G	E		O	D	I	O	U	S
S	O	U	R	I	N	G		O	W	N	U	P	T	O
A	L	B		F	I	R	E	L	I	T		E	O	N
L	I	F	E		D	E	V	O	N		C	R	O	C
A	T	O	M	S		E	E	N		S	A	B	L	E
	H	O	M	E	S	T	R	E	T	C	H			
	T	U	R	K	E	Y	S	H	O	O	T			
	S	A	I	D	T	H	E	W	O	R	D			
K	H	A	K	I		T	I	E		S	T	E	E	D
N	O	R	A		K	H	M	E	R		S	A	F	E
E	R	A		W	H	E	E	L	E	R		S	I	P
W	A	R	H	E	A	D		S	E	A	G	U	L	L
	S	A	B	E	N	A		S	T	E	R	E	O	
	T	O	P	S	Y			S	E	E	D	Y		

46

```
  R E D     S K I F F E D  
S E X E D   D O W N R I V E R
W A T E R   A N A T O L I A N
E L E M I   D E J A   E A R S
D I N   V I A   A C O R N S  
I S S U E S   A L T O        
S T I L L L I F E   P R O V  
H I V E   E L F I N   A L I T
  C E S T   L I N E D R I V E
      A J A X   S O E V E R  
  G A R N E T   S T R   E R N
D O L E   K E M O   E X T R A
S T E E L Y A R D   M E R I T
C O N V U L S E S   I R E N E
  N E E D L E D       S E E  
```

47

```
M O P E D E R S     M I A S  
U N E X O T I C   P E N M E N
S E R E N A T E   E S C U D O
I S I S   S T N I C H O L A S
C H O     E T T U   N E N E  
M A D E   A R S O N I S T S  
A R I S T A S   R I O T      
N E C T A R     A N A D E M  
    E R O O   G R A N O L A  
  D O E S N T P A Y   T M E N
A R A M   I O U S     I M A  
T A R A N T E L L A   A N E T
L I A B L E   S I L I C A N E
I N G L E S   A N I S E T T E
  S E E R     R E A S S E S S
```

48

```
R E A M     E A S T E R E G G
A L D E R   S C H O L A R L Y
G E O D E   T E R R A R I U M
E N R I C H   S E R P E N T S
D A N T E I I I   D I S      
      A S T R A   D E C O C T
P A N T S U I T S   S A M M Y
U G L I   P S H A W   N O O K
N E R V E   H O L E I N O N E
S E B E R G   S U E D E      
      A R C   S K I L I F T  
B O D Y S U R F   S O L V E R
E X A M I N E R S   M O I R A
B E R I N G S E A   S N E A D
E N E R G E T I C     I S L E
```

49

```
S H I M M E R E D   C L A S S
L E T H A L I T Y   L E I L A
A C C O L A D E S   E A R E D
N T H   A T E S   P A R T E D
D A I L I E S   C O N N I V E
E R N E S   P O S S E M E N  
R E G R E S S I V E   R E D S
          S C A L E R S      
A R F S   O V E R S T A F F S
N E U T E R E D     E Y R I E
I G N O R E D   T S A R I N A
M A D R A S   P E A R   G I B
A L I A S   M A S T I C A T E
T I N G E   C A T E N A T E D
E A G E R   C R A S S N E S S
```

50

```
  M C C   N A T H     G A E L
L E A H   A D U E   B I B L E
T A K E I T O R L E A V E I T
D R E W A L O N G B R E A T H
  A S S T     F A R   S M E E
    T E M P O   O S U        
U T A H   E R R S   S P O I L
T A K E S T O T H E S T U M P
E R A S E   W H E E   H I P S
    C A P   E A G R E        
A S H E   R A W     O G R E  
B E I N T O S O M E T H I N G
H A V E A S C R E W L O O S E
O T E R O   O S T E   S T U N
R O S Y     T E A R   T S E  
```

```
E R S E   L A M A R   V I C
L I M I T   I C O N O   A R A
F O U R H U N D R E D   N A M
    E P I C A L       I T A
U R E   A D M   N E T T L E R
F E N E T R E       R O L L O
O N E F R A N C   M O R A Y S
    F I F T Y F O U R
R E J E C T   S A R S E N E T
A N I T A     M O S S I E R
M A T E L O T   I C E   N E Y
P C T     F R E S C A
A T E   O N E T H O U S A N D
G E R   C O N T E   X E N I A
E D S   A D D E D   W A X Y
```

```
    S P O C K   S W I M S
    C H A C H I   W A R I E S T
B R U S H E D   I N A S T I R
L E T T E R M A N     E S T A
O A T E R   A L G E B R A I C
O M E R   N A S A L     I N K
M Y R N A   B E C U R L S
    A R I M A T H E A
  E S K I M O S     S C A R F
S M U   S A N T A   E L E A
E P I C E N T E R   S H E E R
P I T A   A R I S T O T L E
T R I S T A N   S T A R T E D
S E N H O R A   T E N S E D
    G A M I N   A N G E R
```

```
B L A C K B E L T   M A J O R
I V Y L E A G U E   E R A S E
N I N E T Y O N E   S A N T A
    O C H   U N A S L E E P
L O W P H   B L E S T   S O S
A R E A   C O A R S E
V O L T   A Y R   E N T O M B
E N T R A P S   A R T U R O S
R O Y A L S   A G T   R O T I
    L U C I U S   Q U O D
F B I   C L I N E   O U T R E
R E D A L E R T   E N O
E L I S E   C H A S T I S E D
A L O H A   L A Y S A S I D E
K I T E R   E Y E O P E N E R
```

```
F R E E L A N C E   A S P E R
R E S T A R E A S   M O R S E
I N T E R C E P T   E L E C T
E T A S   E D E R   S O N A R
N E T   D E C O R   S A L A
D R E A M   D O G I E   T A C
      H U B   D E V A   A T E
S Q U A R E S   N E S T L E D
T U N   A L T I   R E V
R I D   L O R N A   L A M A S
E X E S   W A T E R   A S P
S O R E S   P E R I   L I S A
S T A V E   P R A G M A T I C
E I G E R   E N T O U R A G E
S C E N E   D E E R S K I N S
```

```
A B J U R E   T R E   A G R A
N O O N E R   H E N R I I I I
T O U T E R   E X T E R N A L
I S L E S     ● A R D S
● T E R E L   L E S   O B E
E S S   S O R E L   T E R A I
      N E A   L A G E R S
  W A I T I N G F O R G O ●
Z E L D A S   L A C
A L L O F   S E N A T   A R A
P L Y   F G H   L E A V E N
    P E R I ●   A G A P E
A Q U A T I N T   E R O T I C
M U S C A T E L   T U R A N ●
P E C K   S S E   S P A R S E
```

56

	M	I	S	L	E	D		S	U	P	R	A
B	E	D	T	I	M	E		H	E	N	R	I	S
A	T	E	I	N	T	O		P	E	A	C	O	C	K
D	R	O	N	E			I	N	T	O	N	E	S
V	O	L	K	S	W	A	G	E	N	B	U	G	
I	D	O	S		I	C	U		Y	A	T	
B	O	G		C	L	I	N	G		C	H	A	S	M
E	M	U		R	E	D	B	O	O	K		N	E	O
S	E	E	D	Y		S	O	R	B	S		D	X	L
		I	O	S		A	G	E		N	O	T	A
	C	O	M	P	U	T	E	R	V	I	R	U	S	
L	A	U	R	E	L	S			E	A	R	P	S
E	R	R	A	T	I	C		P	E	R	C	A	L	E
K	I	S	M	E	T		E	R	M	I	N	E	S
S	P	E	A	R			G	A	I	N	S	T	

57

S	A	U	K		B	I	A	S		S	T	R	O	P
O	L	L	A		O	N	C	E		E	R	O	S	E
D	I	S	P	R	O	V	E	D		R	U	N	I	N
S	E	T	L	I	N	E		U	N	E	N	D	E	D
	N	E	A	T	E	N		C	I	N	D	E	R	S
E	A	R	N	E	S	T		E	V	E	L		
A	T	M				R	E	L	E	N	T	S
S	O	A	P	I	E	R		S	N	Y	D	E	R	S
E	R	N	E	S	T	O				F	A	T
		S	O	H	O		P	I	G	P	E	N	S
B	E	A	T	L	E	S		O	G	L	E	R	S	
O	X	H	E	A	R	T		M	O	U	N	T	E	D
A	P	O	R	T		E	S	O	T	E	R	I	C	A
R	E	L	E	E		R	A	N	I		O	T	T	S
S	L	E	D	S		S	L	A	T		D	I	S	H

58

S	P	E	E	D	S		S	C	A	L	A	W	A	G
P	A	T	T	O	N		H	A	R	A	K	I	R	I
A	L	C	O	V	E		A	N	I	M	A	T	E	D
C	O	E		E	L	E	N	A	S		H	O	G
E	A	T		S	L	O	G		E	N	S	I	L	E
B	L	E	B			S	H	E		A	E	T	A	T
A	T	R	E	U	S		A	R	E	T	E		
R	O	A	D	T	O	S	I	N	G	A	P	O	R	E
		L	I	T	H	E		G	L	I	D	E	R
S	U	M	A	C		A	X	E		N	O	T	A
L	L	A	M	A	S		P	L	U	S		M	I	S
I	T	S			M	A	R	S	H	A		E	N	A
D	I	S	P	R	O	V	E		H	O	T	T	U	B
E	M	I	R	A	T	E	S		U	N	R	E	E	L
S	A	F	E	N	E	S	S		H	E	A	R	S	E

59

F	O	R	T	K	N	O	X			A	R	C	A	
O	V	E	R	E	A	S	Y		A	V	O	U	C	H
R	E	V	E	R	S	A	L		B	A	M	B	O	O
G	R	E	E	N	A	G	E		S	N	A	I	L	S
O	A	R			E	M	M	E	T		C	Y	T
E	L	I	C	I	T			I	N	G	R	A	T	E
S	L	E	E	V	E		E	N	T	A	I	L	E	D
		C	Y	L	I	N	D	E	R	S		
B	E	S	I	L	E	N	T		E	D	E	M	A	S
U	S	E	L	E	S	S		S	E	S	A	M	E
R	T	E		A	C	T	A	S			S	M	A
G	R	I	N	G	O		S	T	A	G	E	S	E	T
L	I	N	E	U	P		C	O	G	I	T	A	T	E
E	N	T	R	E	E		A	V	E	R	A	G	E	R
	S	O	I	R			P	E	D	D	L	E	R	S

60

W	R	E	C	K	A	G	E		T	E	A	R	S	
H	A	S	H	O	V	E	R		E	C	L	A	I	R
I	N	C	U	B	A	T	E		N	O	T	I	C	E
S	T	A	T	E			C	P	A		I	N	K	S
T	A	P	E		A	T	T	A	C	K		F	E	E
	N	E	S	T	L	E		P	E	N	D	A	N	T
			U	L	N	A			I	D	L	E	S
	J	E	R	R	Y	S	E	I	N	F	E	L	D	
S	A	X	O	N			C	R	E	E		
E	L	I	T	I	S	M		A	S	S	E	S	S	
D	O	G		N	I	E	C	E	S		N	E	E	D
A	P	E	D		E	A	R			M	A	M	I	E
N	I	N	E	R	S		O	P	T	I	M	I	Z	E
S	E	C	R	E	T		F	E	R	R	E	T	E	D
	S	E	N	T	A		T	R	E	E	L	E	S	S

C	H	A	R	L	E	S	I	I	▮	D	A	C	C	A
L	O	S	E	A	T	U	R	N	▮	A	R	R	A	S
A	M	Y	F	I	S	H	E	R	▮	D	O	E	R	S
M	I	L	E	R	▮	A	N	O	A	▮	M	A	L	O
P	L	U	R	▮	C	R	E	A	M	▮	A	M	I	N
S	Y	M	▮	P	O	T	S	D	A	M	▮	P	T	A
▮	▮	H	E	R	O	▮	S	T	A	T	I	O	N	▮
A	S	C	E	N	D	▮	▮	E	R	N	E	S	T	▮
B	E	A	R	C	U	B	▮	B	U	N	T	▮	▮	▮
R	A	M	▮	E	R	A	S	U	R	E	▮	C	U	P
O	L	P	E	▮	O	K	A	Y	S	▮	M	E	G	A
G	A	I	N	▮	Y	E	N	S	▮	F	A	R	A	S
A	N	E	A	R	▮	O	D	O	M	E	T	E	R	S
T	E	S	T	Y	▮	F	R	U	S	T	R	A	T	E
E	S	T	E	E	▮	F	A	T	T	A	I	L	E	D

S	T	R	E	T	C	H	▮	▮	T	S	P	▮	▮	▮
T	R	E	M	O	L	O	S	▮	R	A	I	T	T	S
J	I	V	E	T	A	L	K	▮	U	N	C	O	A	T
A	V	E	▮	E	R	E	I	▮	▮	H	O	O	K	A
M	I	R	▮	R	E	D	I	D	▮	E	T	H	E	R
E	A	S	T	▮	▮	N	E	R	D	▮	O	C	T	▮
S	L	E	E	P	I	N	G	C	A	R	▮	T	A	S
▮	P	S	E	U	D	O	L	O	G	I	S	T	S	▮
B	U	C	▮	P	E	T	E	R	I	N	G	O	U	T
O	R	O	▮	P	A	S	S	▮	▮	T	H	A	I	▮
U	S	U	R	Y	▮	O	S	A	G	E	▮	A	L	T
R	U	R	A	L	▮	O	R	A	L	▮	N	T	H	▮
G	I	S	M	O	S	▮	N	E	V	E	R	D	I	E
S	T	E	E	V	E	▮	S	N	I	V	E	L	E	R
▮	▮	N	E	W	▮	▮	O	N	E	N	E	S	S	▮

▮	M	I	R	A	C	L	E	M	I	L	E	▮
▮	B	A	T	H	R	O	O	M	S	C	A	L	E
N	O	N	T	O	T	A	L	I	T	A	R	I	A	N
O	N	A	▮	S	T	I	R	▮	R	A	S	T	A
T	A	C	O	S	▮	E	T	A	G	E	▮	H	E	R
F	I	L	U	M	▮	D	A	T	E	▮	R	A	N	K
A	R	E	T	E	S	▮	S	E	N	T	A	▮
R	E	D	B	A	I	T	▮	S	T	O	M	P	E	R
▮	▮	U	L	N	A	R	▮	S	T	O	O	G	E
D	O	R	Y	▮	A	S	I	A	▮	A	N	T	O	N
A	C	E	▮	H	I	M	O	M	▮	L	A	B	I	A
D	A	V	A	O	▮	A	R	A	B	▮	E	S	T
A	L	E	S	S	A	N	D	R	O	V	O	L	T	A
▮	A	R	T	E	S	I	A	N	W	E	L	L	S	▮
▮	T	I	N	P	A	N	A	L	L	E	Y	▮

▮	R	A	N	G	▮	T	E	M	P	L	A	T	E
F	E	R	A	L	▮	T	I	D	E	S	O	V	E	R
O	F	T	E	A	▮	R	A	I	N	C	O	A	T	S
R	E	M	▮	S	P	I	R	E	S	▮	K	N	E	E
A	R	U	▮	S	A	R	A	S	▮	P	E	T	S	▮
L	E	S	A	B	R	E	S	▮	S	A	D	▮
O	N	E	R	O	O	M	▮	T	R	U	M	P	S	▮
S	C	U	T	T	L	E	▮	P	R	E	P	A	R	E
S	E	M	I	T	E	▮	L	I	N	T	I	E	R	▮
▮	▮	C	O	E	▮	C	O	T	T	O	N	T	O	▮
S	L	U	M	▮	C	A	T	C	H	▮	T	E	T	▮
S	A	I	L	▮	A	L	L	T	H	E	▮	E	R	I
P	R	O	A	C	T	I	V	E	▮	S	U	N	I	N
C	O	N	T	A	I	N	E	D	▮	E	M	O	T	E
A	S	S	E	R	T	E	D	▮	S	A	N	S	▮

R	E	N	E	G	E	S	▮	F	A	R	O	E	S	E
O	V	E	R	A	C	T	▮	I	P	E	C	A	C	S
M	A	T	A	D	O	R	▮	G	L	A	S	S	E	S
A	L	T	▮	S	L	U	S	H	E	D	▮	E	P	A
N	U	L	L	▮	E	M	P	T	Y	▮	C	O	T	Y
S	N	E	A	D	▮	P	A	S	▮	P	O	U	R	S
▮	A	D	M	I	R	E	R	▮	D	A	N	T	E	▮
▮	▮	B	R	I	T	T	L	E	S	T	▮
▮	R	H	E	T	T	▮	A	I	R	H	E	A	D	▮
S	H	I	N	Y	▮	P	C	S	▮	A	N	T	E	S
C	E	R	T	▮	B	O	U	T	S	▮	D	E	B	I
U	N	A	▮	H	I	S	S	I	N	G	▮	L	U	G
B	I	B	L	I	K	E	▮	N	O	U	R	I	S	H
A	S	L	A	V	E	R	▮	G	R	A	Y	E	S	T
S	H	E	K	E	L	S	▮	S	T	M	A	R	Y	S

66

```
H A T I N H A N D █ A D E P T
I V Y L E A G U E █ N I X I E
F I R S T L A D Y █ D A C C A
I D E A L I Z E █ S I M O O M
█ █ █ O D E █ T O R O N T O █
B R O W S E █ C O D O N █ █ █
L I M O S █ M O M A N D P O P
A G A R █ N O R M S █ J I V E
H A R D C A N D Y █ V I P E R
█ S H I E S █ C E M E N T █ █
K U M Q U A T █ M A R █ █ █ █
A R O U N D █ P O N I E D U P
P I S A N █ S O L I T A I R E
O C H R E █ A L A N A R K I N
W H E E L █ M A R E S N E S T
```

67

```
G L A S S ᴱʸᴱ █ L O A █ D I V A
B E S T O W █ T R I P E D A L
S N O R R I █ D I S R A E L I
█ S P A R T A █ N O D O U S █
█ P E N N A M E █ ᴱʸᴱ L E T █
A P T █ L E N T O █ I D O █ █
L A R F █ S E E N █ D I G I T
A G A I N S T █ O P A C I T Y
S E N S E █ T E R R █ K E E P
█ S H E █ E M A I L █ S R O █
P O P ᴱʸᴱ █ E S T I V A L █ █
S M I L A X █ L A R E D O █ █
H E R E W I T H █ T R I O D E
A G E N E S I S █ E U C L I D
W A D S █ T U T █ ᴱʸᴱ P A T C H
```

68

```
S T A L E M A T E S █ R O B B
C A P I T U L A N T █ E C R U
A P P L E S A U C E █ L E E S
T I E █ E R R █ E M I L E S
T O A D █ M I C R O C O D E
E C L A T █ N O H I T T E R
D A S H E R █ E L I █ S R S
█ S E E M █ A D E S █ █
F R A █ H O C █ E S T O P S
R E L A T E T O █ P E A R Y
O V E R R A T E D █ S T A R
M E R G E R █ V I P █ M I I
A L T O █ S P A C E O P E R A
G E E S █ A L L T E R R A I N
E D D Y █ L O S A N G E L E S
```

69

```
M O O N O V E R P A R A D O R
A L T E R O N E S C O U R S E
H E A R T O F D A R K N E S S
A G R O █ D O Y L E █ T W I T
L S U █ F O R E M A N █ S E E
█ B L O C █ I G E T █
A N A L Y S E █ C E M E N T S
B U N D T █ █ E X I S T
A N A G R A M █ P E S T L E S
█ S A M E █ L O I S █
C D R █ P A T R O L S █ B B C
P R I M █ T H E E I █ R O L L
L O V E L E A D S T H E W A Y
U P A R O U N D T H E B E N D
S A L E S R E S I S T A N C E
```

70

```
█ S A M O S █ T O G A S █
T O P K I C K █ M E N I S C I
O N E A D A Y █ E X U L T E D
A F C █ L L A M A S █ A P E
T I T S █ A A R O N █ R I T A
E L E C T █ B M I █ O R E L
E E R I E R █ A R B I T E R S
█ S A O █ A G A █
Q U I S L I N G █ V O T A R Y
U N D O █ O A F █ T E P E E
A M O R █ M I L O S █ D O G S
V O L █ N O S T R A █ L A M
E V I L O N E █ M U D H O L E
R E Z O N E S █ A N T I G E N
█ D E C O Y █ T A S T Y █
```

71

```
A B A C I   W E I R   B A N S
S O L O N   A P S E   A W O L
T A I N T   RR EE EE DD   R A B E
A C A D E M E S   E T O I L E
      O R A N   O N E S T E P
A L A R I C   I N S E T
BB EE DD   M A I N S   M A T T E S
O R E M   U L C E R   T E E T H
T Y R O L   E A T A T   AA R E
      L O O N S   C R A M M E D
M A L D I V E   G E A R
E Q U I N E   H A R D C O R E
L U C E   RR OO OO MM   E A S E L
D A I S   A N K A   I R A N I
S E A T   N A Y S   N O Y E S
```

72

```
  L E M M A     C A D I Z
T I M E O F F   A M A T I S
I N I T I A L   R E N E G E S
B E L A   R A Z I N G   Z I P
I D Y L L   M I B   M A I Z E
      S O B I G     E L G A R
A Z O   D A N Z A     A L B S
R U N   Z A G A Z I G   A L E
I G E T   O G I V E   R E D
E Z R A S     G N O M E
T W O T O   E E G   S M A R T
T A U   M E L D E D   O B I E
A N S W E R S   R E S T I V E
  G L O R I A   S E C E D E D
    Y E S E S   R I D E R
```

73

```
E M B R Y O S   A L S M I T H
M A R I A N A   N A T A S H A
F R E A K E D   O V E R S O W
O C E L O T   K N E E J E R K
R O Z   V O L E   L O I N S
S P E C   N O P L A C E
T O D O S   S T A L L   E S T
E L I Z A B E T H T A Y L O R
R O N   V I T R O   D E C C A
      R E B O A R D   P A I N
S P I E S   C E O S   P A S
K I N S F O L K   D E F I L E
O N L E A V E   P O L I T I C
S T A N C E S   B E L F A S T
H O Y D E N S   A S S E N T S
```

74

```
  S H E R P A   N O R M A L
S H A D I E R   O V E R L A Y
M A Z E P P A   V I Z C A Y A
O P I N E S   M O N A   B A H
K E N S   I R A T E   K A N T
E R G   E C O L E   G O M E Z
    F L O U T   F O R A G E
A R T I C L E   D E R A N G E
P E O R I A   S I R E N
O G L E D   S T E R N   M A W
L I E D   A C U T E   T A T A
L O R   B L O B   T H U M B S
O N A T E A R   F O O T M E N
S A T I A T E   D U E E A S T
  L E N D E R   A T R E S T
```

75

```
P O N D E R O S A   A M A S S
U N O R G A N I C   C O R E A
R A T I O N A L E   T I T A N
S I T E   T N T   H O L I S M
E R O S E     I T A R   C H A
      T A S T E R S   T H O R
S D I   S H A R I S   L O R I
T I N Y T I M   S L I C K E N
A S T A   F A T T E N   E S O
L U R K   T R I E S T E
I N I   K E A N   O L D A S
N I C K E D   W E T   M U N I
I T A L Y   C A N O N I C A L
S E T A E   A R O M A R A M A
T R E N D   D E L E G A T E S
```